FOUR-STAR PROOFREADING

Kendall Hunt
publishing company

Julia Laffoon-Jackson

Cover images © Shutterstock.com

www.kendallhunt.com
Send all inquiries to:
4050 Westmark Drive
Dubuque, IA 52004-1840

Published in the United States of America

DEDICATION

To all of my students:

Past students for encouraging me to write this book

Present students for using and appreciating it

Future students for inspiring me to improve it

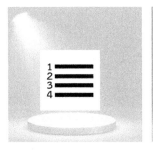

CONTENTS

Chapter 3: Separating Items in a List 67

Chapter 4: Separating Extra Information from the Main Thought 97

Chapter 5: Proofreading Your Final Draft 133

Appendix: Reviewing Quick Guides 141

ACKNOWLEDGEMENTS

For their love and support, I wish to thank my husband, Bill, and my daughters, Briana and Savanna. For their vitally important feedback throughout various drafts of this book, I am thankful for two groups of people: colleagues at Hopkinsville Community College, Brian Coatney, Stephanie Holt, Amanda Sauermann, and Martha White; and fellow writers of the Hanson Writers' Workshop, Robin Daniels, Tim Frasier, and John Laffoon. For bringing this book to fruition, I am grateful for my publishing team at Kendall Hunt: Torrie Johnson, Nicole Mathers, and Jennifer Wreisner.

INTRODUCTION

Preparing to Proofread

After reading this brief introduction, you should be able to do the following:

- Understand when and why you should proofread your writings.
- Determine if your current writing assignment is ready for the proofreading process.
- Determine which chapters are applicable to your current skill level.

Why Should You Proofread?

It's midnight, and the final draft of your paper is due tomorrow morning at 8:00. As a conscientious student, you followed your English professor's instructions to write and revise multiple drafts during the past weeks. You made your point, developed it thoroughly, and organized the supporting details logically. You corrected those squiggly underlined areas that your computer program noted as errors, yet you are still worried.

"Be sure you proofread your paper before submitting it," your professor had cautioned the class. Uncertain how proofreading is any different from the revising that you have already done, you sigh as you pick up your paper. You read through it aloud one last time but are unable to find additional errors. Promptly at 8:00 the next morning, you submit your final draft and pray that your professor finds nothing wrong with it.

One long, worried-filled week passes. Then your worst nightmare comes true. Your professor returns your paper—bleeding with red ink. You wonder how she managed to find dozens of errors in places where you found none, and you suspect she invented rules as she was grading just to see how many red ink pens she could use up on your paper. You also wonder about all the grammar and punctuation rules that she says you ignored. What purpose do they serve? Why are there so many, and why are they so complex? Your biggest concern, though, is to find out how to proofread your remaining essay assignments so that you can make a passing grade in the course.

You ask your classmates who made *A*'s for proofreading tips. They answer, "Just read your paper aloud to see if you have any mistakes left." Their advice is the same as what your English handbook had recommended and exactly what you had done, but that method did not work for you. Discouraged, you consider dropping the course. This, however, is not the time to give up; instead, it is time to work through this book.

Four-Stage Proofreading explains a simple yet effective way to proofread your own essays and is designed specifically for student writers and others who struggle with proofreading their own work. Each stage in this system is easy to follow and yields a number of benefits.

First of all, the four-stage proofreading system empowers you. Not only will you learn how to proofread, but you will also learn why you are using this particular method. This knowledge places you in full control of correcting your own writing.

Second, this proofreading system helps you look at every sentence of your paper in isolation from the rest of the sentences. Forced isolation of each sentence is the most effective proofreading technique you can employ to find your own errors because it allows you to judge each sentence on its own merit. Additionally, you will learn what questions to ask in order to judge each sentence accurately.

A third benefit to this proofreading system is that it removes the mystery and complexity of punctuation. You will learn the three major reasons behind the rules of punctuation, not merely the rules themselves. Once you gain this knowledge, you will begin thinking like the professional writer that you are becoming.

Finally, following this system will help you attain the results you desire. You will have greater self-confidence in your writing and proofreading abilities. Plus, you will be able to earn higher grades than you would have without this system. Ultimately, moreover, your papers will be clearer and will communicate effectively to your readers—and that, of course, is the whole point of writing.

When Should You Proofread?

Proofreading is the final stage of the writing process. To determine if you are ready to begin proofreading, answer the following questions about your current writing assignment.

	Yes	No
1. Does your paper follow the instructions your professor gave you?	❏	❏
2. Is your main idea clear?	❏	❏
3. Does your paper follow a clear pattern of organization?	❏	❏
4. Did you set it aside for a day or two after writing it?	❏	❏

5. Did you revise it with convincing supporting details?   ❏   ❏

6. Did you set it aside for a day or two after revising it?   ❏   ❏

7. Did you revise it yet again?   ❏   ❏

8. Have you corrected every mistake you and your computer program were able to detect?   ❏   ❏

If you answered no to any of the questions above, you are not yet ready to begin the proofreading process. First, take the time to complete all of the steps outlined in the above questions before proceeding.

Which Chapters Should You Work?

If your professor assigns four different writings that build on one basic skill at a time, then you should work through the appropriate chapter for each writing assignment:

Chapter	Skill Focus
1	Avoiding Fragments
2	Avoiding Run-on Sentences
3	Punctuating Items in a List
4	Punctuating Sentences

Each of the above chapters provides valuable information and a series of progressive exercises to increase your understanding of clear and purposeful writing (observations), to practice newly-gained skills that will prepare you for proofreading (preparations), and to equip you to effectively proofread final drafts (applications).

If your professor requires that you avoid all errors beginning with your first writing assignment, then you should work through Chapter 5. This chapter explains the four stages of the proofreading system and guides you through your final draft step-by-step. As you do so, it will direct you to the specific chapter(s) that you need to read and work in order to address your particular errors.

Practicing the four-stage proofreading system described in this book is critical to your success as a writer. Once you have become familiar with the information in the chapters and have employed this proofreading system on several papers, you will find the Quick Guides at the back of the book helpful. Refer to them as needed in your future college courses and in your future career.

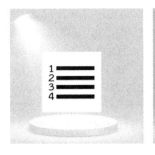   

CHAPTER 1

Ending a Complete Thought

In this chapter, you will learn how to proofread your papers to make every sentence a complete thought. After you have successfully worked through this chapter, you should be able to do the following:

- Identify the five essential elements of every sentence.
- Distinguish between complete and incomplete sentences.
- Evaluate writings to determine if incomplete sentences exist.
- Apply proofreading techniques to make every sentence complete.

Identifying Fragments

When you were a young child learning to read and write, you discovered that the period signals to readers that they have reached the end of a sentence. In fact, letting readers know when a complete thought has ended is the primary purpose of punctuation. If a writer makes the mistake of placing a period after an incomplete thought, the readers will be confused.

While acceptable in advertisements and in conversations, incomplete thoughts are not acceptable in academic writing and in business writing. In a conversation, the speaker can immediately answer any questions the listener may have. A writer cannot. In an advertisement, a picture completes the thought for the readers. For example, suppose we see a billboard with only two words on it: *Refreshingly delicious*. By itself, this is an incomplete thought. Accompanied by a picture of a specific food or drink, we are able to complete the thought. As a writer, you must express yourself clearly by writing only complete thoughts and ending those thoughts with periods.

An incomplete thought disguised as a sentence is called a fragment.

Fragment: Watching the sun set.

Fragment: People watching the sun set.

Fragment: As they watched the sun set.

At first glance, the above three thoughts look like sentences since they each start with a capital letter and end with a period. A careful reading, however, reveals that they are incomplete and do not make sense by themselves. They contain only fragments of a sentence instead of all the necessary parts that make up a sentence.

Because fragments communicate ineffectively (or not at all), readers have to guess what parts are missing and what the writer should have written. For this reason, college professors in all disciplines—not just English—deduct several points from a paper when they come across a fragment. Therefore, you want to ensure that each sentence in your final draft is truly a complete thought.

Depending upon what your instructor assigned, your final draft consists of either a single paragraph or a multi-paragraph essay. Each paragraph consists of multiple sentences, and each one is a complete thought—or is it? By the end of this chapter, you may be surprised to discover that some of your statements are not complete thoughts at all. If that is the case, you will need to change them into true sentences in order to communicate effectively to your readers.

Correcting Fragments

Beginning a thought with a capital letter and ending it with a period are not the only characteristics of a sentence. To qualify as a sentence, all five of the following parts must be present:

- a **capital letter** starting the sentence
- a **subject** telling who or what the sentence is about
- a **verb** showing that the subject exists or is doing something
- a **complete thought** giving the sentence meaning
- a **period** (or **question mark**) ending the sentence (or question)

The next few sections of this chapter explain how to identify subjects, verbs, and complete thoughts. In addition, you will learn how to correct fragments by adding the missing parts. Finally, prepared with this knowledge, you will be able to find and correct fragments in your own writing through the four-stage proofreading process.

ADDING A SUBJECT

One of the five parts that every sentence must have is a subject. The subject is the noun or pronoun that tells who or what the sentence is about. Additionally, the subject is the noun or pronoun that is doing something (for example, writing, talking, or existing). Nouns and pronouns name people, places, objects, or concepts.

Every person, every place, every object, and every concept that you can think of is a noun, and all nouns have the *potential* to be the subject of a sentence. Listed below are just a few:

People: Kristen, students, professor

Places: Massachusetts, Wal-Mart, college

Objects: essay, car, books

Concepts: freedom, independence, joy

OBSERVATION 1

Directions:

Underline all of the nouns in the sentences below. The number in red tells how many nouns are in each sentence.

Example:

A <u>noun</u> is a <u>person</u>, <u>place</u>, <u>object</u>, or <u>concept</u>. *5*

1. The beautiful flowers brought tears of joy to her eyes. *4*

2. Mia revised her paper each day for two weeks. *4*

3. Two experts have opposing views on the issue. *3*

4. After three weeks of dating, the couple eloped in Las Vegas. *4*

5. A young horse won the race. *2*

Now to determine which noun is the subject of a sentence, ask this question: which noun is doing something?

Example: The <u>student</u> worked on her <u>paper</u> for two <u>weeks</u>.

In the above example, all the nouns are underlined, but only one tells who is doing something: *student*. Therefore, the subject is *student*.

OBSERVATION 2

Directions:

1. Go back to Observation 1.

2. Write the letter *S* for subject over the noun that is doing something.

Example:

> *S*
> A <u>noun</u> consists of a <u>person</u>, <u>place</u>, <u>thing</u>, or <u>concept</u>. *5*

The subject of a sentence can also be a pro**noun**, which is simply a noun substitute. However, while not every noun is the subject of a sentence, subject pronouns are subjects automatically. Also, in contrast to the vast number of nouns, there are only eight subject pronouns.

Subject Pronouns of People	Subject Pronouns of Places, Objects, and Concepts
I	it
we	they
he	
she	
they	
who	

Take a look at the following two sentences:

Example: <u>She</u> worked on her <u>paper</u> for two <u>weeks</u>.

Example: <u>It</u> is crowded with excited <u>people</u>.

The nouns and the subject pronouns in the two examples above are underlined. In the first one, the pronoun *she* tells who is doing something; therefore, it is the subject of the sentence. In the second example, the pronoun *it* tells what is doing something; therefore it is the subject of the sentence.

OBSERVATION 3

Directions:

1. Circle the subject pronoun in each sentence and write the letter *S* for subject over it.

2. Underline all of the nouns in each sentence. The number of nouns is in red.

S

(It) will be the <u>subject</u> of the <u>sentence</u>. *2*

1. They met early in the morning to go to the appointment. *2*

2. As a favor, she drove Will to the building in an old car. *4*

3. Unfortunately, it had a flat tire on the way to the meeting. *3*

4. As a result, he missed his appointment with the executives. *3*

5. We need to replace the tire and put gas in the car. *3*

Sometimes more than one noun or subject pronoun will be the subjects of a sentence.

Example: <u>Bill</u> and <u>I</u> live in a small <u>town</u> with only one traffic <u>light</u>.

The three nouns and one subject pronoun are underlined. Who is doing something? The answer is two people are living: *Bill* and *I*. Therefore, both of these words are the subjects of the sentence.

OBSERVATION 4

Directions:

1. Underline all of the subject pronouns and all of the nouns in the sentences below. The total number of words to underline is in red.

2. Write the letter *S* over both the subject pronoun and the noun that tell who or what is doing something.

Example:

S   *S*

<u>Bill</u> and <u>I</u> live in a small <u>town</u> with one traffic <u>light</u>.   *4*

1. She and Jeremy understand the difference between nouns and pronouns.   *5*

2. Oliver and he are roommates in this dorm.   *4*

3. They and their instructor are going on a field trip to the planetarium.   *4*

4. Next Saturday, my family and I will take a vacation in the mountains.   *5*

5. Before the tornado, we and our neighbors took refuge in our basements.   *5*

The next section covers an easier way to determine the subject of the sentence.

IGNORING PREPOSITIONAL PHRASES

An easier way to determine which noun is the subject of a sentence is to ignore all nouns at the end of every prepositional phrase. Those nouns cannot be the subject of a sentence, but the remaining noun(s) will be the subject.

A prepositional phrase starts with a preposition (see the box of prepositions) and ends with a noun or pronoun. Any noun or pronoun that ends a prepositional phrase is **not** the subject of a sentence because it is the **object** of a preposition. Therefore, you can ignore or cross out all prepositional phrases.

Of course, before you can cross them out, you must be able to recognize a preposition every time you see one. Study the box of prepositions for a few minutes. What feature do most of them have in common?

BOX OF PREPOSITIONS

A	B	D	E	F
aboard	before	despite	except	for
about	behind	down		from
above	below	during		
across	beneath			
after	beside			
against	between			
along	beyond			
among	by			
around				
at				

I	L	N	O	P
in	like	near	of	past
into		next to	off	
inside			on	
			out	
			outside	
			over	

T	U	W		
through	under	with		
throughout	underneath	within		
to	until	without		
toward	up			
towards	upon			

As you can see, most prepositions indicate position or direction. (The preposition *of* is an exception.) An easy way to remember prepositional phrases is to think of positions a mouse can go to when it approaches a group of houses.

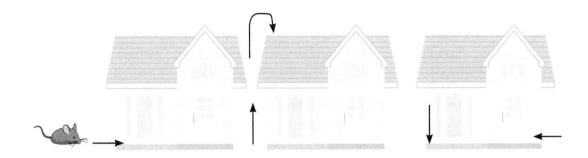

in a house	under the ground
around a house	to the house
between two houses	through a window
among three houses	out the door
on the roof	from the house

Once you cross out prepositional phrases, you will not have many words left.

Example: The little gray mouse ran ~~under the door~~ ~~into the house~~ and then scrambled ~~out of the first window~~.

In the example above, all the prepositional phrases are crossed out because the nouns at the end of them cannot contain the subject. Only one of the remaining words is a noun: *mouse*. Therefore, the subject of the sentence is mouse.

Likewise, in the next two examples, the prepositional phrases are crossed out (since they cannot contain the subject), and the nouns and pronouns that are left are underlined.

Example: ~~In the morning~~, the <u>students</u> must submit their final <u>drafts</u> ~~to the teacher~~.

Example: <u>They</u> wrote <u>essays</u> ~~on various topics~~.

Is the first sentence about the students or their drafts? Who is doing something? The answer is that the *students* are doing something. Therefore, the subject is *students*. Is the second sentence about *they* or *essays*? Who is doing something? The answer is *they* did the writing, so the subject is *they*.

OBSERVATION 1

Directions:

1. Cross out all the prepositional phrases.

2. Underline the remaining nouns.

3. Write *S* for subject above the noun that tells who or what the sentence is about.

Example:

S
The <u>man</u> ~~in the suit~~ is the college <u>president</u>.

1. The student in the orange shirt is in my English class.

2. Jillian parked her car next to a silver Prius.

3. The students at this college must spend a lot of time on their homework.

4. Prepositional phrases begin with a preposition and end with an object.

5. Of course, subjects are not found in prepositional phrases.

OBSERVATION 2

Directions:

1. Cross out all prepositional phrases.

2. Underline the nouns and subject pronouns that you did not cross out.

3. Write *S* for subject above the subject pronoun or noun that tells who or what is doing something.

$$S$$

Lying ~~on my desk at home~~ is my final <u>draft</u>.

1. In the future, she may invent a more accurate system for computers to detect errors in writing.

2. For the next several months, motorists can expect gasoline prices to rise.

3. The turn signal on this vehicle is on the right side of the steering wheel.

4. On Friday evenings, he plays pickleball at the new court with his friends from work.

5. She is buried under a stack of essays.

Because a subject tells who or what a sentence is about, every sentence must have one. With the prepositional phrases crossed out, you can readily tell when a subject is missing.

Fragment: Covered ~~in a sea of red ink~~.

If you come across a group of words disguised as a sentence but missing a subject (as in the example above), it is a fragment and needs to be changed into a complete sentence. To correct this type of fragment, add the missing subject and any other words necessary to make it a complete sentence.

$$S$$

Correct: Her paper is covered in a sea of red ink.

PREPARATION 1

Directions:

1. Cross out all prepositional phrases.

2. Add a subject and any other words needed to change each fragment into a sentence.

Example:

She
Revised the essay ~~for two weeks~~.
^

1. Faces many challenges at school and at work.

2. Works twelve-hour shifts at night on the third floor of the hospital.

3. Then going to college and sitting in classes for four hours.

4. And goes home to sleep for a few hours before going back to work.

5. Is hard on him physically and mentally.

Why do people write fragments like the type in the previous exercise? When writing a paragraph, they usually have a subject in an earlier sentence but then leave it out in later ones because they mistakenly believe that it is obvious they are still writing about the same subject. However, readers seldom look at an incomplete sentence and declare, "Oh, the subject is obvious. It was stated further up in the paragraph." Instead, they are more likely to look at an incomplete sentence and grumble, "What the heck is this writer talking about?" Like cell phone carriers that do not allow their customers to have roll-over minutes from month to month, readers do not allow writers to have roll-over subjects from sentence to sentence. Every single sentence must state the subject.

PREPARATION 2

Some of the sentences below are complete, but others are incomplete.

Directions:

1. Cross out all prepositional phrases.

2. If it is a complete sentence, underline the subject.

3. If there is no subject, add a subject and any other words needed to change the fragment into a complete sentence.

Examples:

There is a <u>book</u> ~~in the attic~~.

It is covered
~~C~~overed ~~with dust~~.
^

1. The heirs to the estate found some valuable jewelry in the master bedroom.

2. Stored inside a wooden chest under the table.

3. There were two matching necklaces in large, velvet boxes.

4. Made of an enormous sapphire surrounded by white diamonds.

5. Worth at least $5,000 on the wholesale market and $10,000 in jewelry stores.

While it is not too difficult to spot missing subjects in isolated sentences, it is trickier to find a fragment buried inside a paragraph. To do so, you still cross out prepositional phrases. In addition, you will intentionally isolate each group of words punctuated as a sentence to determine whether or not it is complete and can stand alone. To do this forced isolation, read the last sentence in the paragraph first and then read the next-to-last sentence. Continue in this manner until you read the first sentence last.

PREPARATION 3

Directions:

1. Cross out the prepositional phrases.

2. Starting with the last sentence and ending with the first, read each one to see if it has a subject.

3. If there is a subject, underline it.

4. If there is not a subject, add a subject and any other words needed to change the fragment into a complete thought.

Example:

<u>It</u> is c
There is a <u>book</u> <s>in the attic</s>. <s>C</s>overed <s>with dust</s>.
^

Maria attended the first day of classes in the fall semester. Wondering about her classmates. Worried about their opinions. Would they think she was too old to go to college? Encouraging or discouraging? In her first class, there were two other women around her age. In her second class, almost half of the students were older. By noon, she realized college was for students of all ages.

ADDING A VERB

Another essential element that every sentence must have is a verb. A verb tells us what the subject is doing, which may be simply existing.

Example: Darius <u>is</u> here.

Example: Darius <u>plays</u> basketball every afternoon.

In the first example, the verb *is* shows the reader that the subject (Darius) exists. In the second example, the verb *plays* shows the reader that the subject is doing something.

Besides showing that the subject exists or is doing something, verbs are the only words that can change time from past to present to future tense.

Past Tense: The student **was** in class yesterday.

Present Tense: The student **is** in class today.

© Sean K/Shutterstock.com

Future Tense: The student **will be** in class tomorrow.

Past Tense: The teacher **covered** the paper in red ink.

Present Tense: The teacher **covers** the paper in red ink.

Future Tense: The teacher **will cover** the paper in red ink.

Before looking for the verb, first determine the subject by eliminating any prepositional phrases.

Example: The man ~~in the yellow hat and sunglasses~~ has a headache.

Since the sentence is about the *man, man* is the subject.

To find the verb, look at the remaining words left in the sentence. Which one can be changed to a different tense? Only the word *has* (present tense) can be changed to *had* (past tense) or *will have* (future tense). Therefore, *has* is the verb.

If you think that you have found the verb in a sentence but are not positive, try changing that word to a different tense. If you cannot change its form, it is not the verb.

OBSERVATION 1

Directions:

1. Cross out prepositional phrases.

2. Underline the subject once and the verb twice.

Example:

The <u>students</u> <u><u>turned</u></u> in their final drafts.

1. Sonya wrote a lengthy paper on the effects of social networking.

2. Every sentence has a verb inside it.

3. On Monday nights, Steven attends a biology lab at the college.

4. During one lab session, he and his classmates dissected cats.

5. He became nauseous.

Verbs often include more than one word, as in the following example.

Example: The students have been revising their essays for two weeks.

Before looking for the verb, first determine the subject by eliminating any prepositional phrases.

Example: The students have been revising their essays for two weeks.

Since the noun *students* is the word that is doing something, *students* is the subject. Now, which words indicate what the subject is doing? The answer is *have been revising*. All three of those words together form a verb phrase. We can take that verb phrase and change it to other verb tenses as well:

> did revise
> will revise
> revised
> may have been revising
> should have revised
> are revising

Again, only verbs can change their form to other tenses. No other words can change their time.

OBSERVATION 2

Directions:

Change the verbs below into two different tenses of your choosing.

Example:

	will be	<u>is</u>	<u>should have been</u>
1. wrote		_____	_____
2. attends		_____	_____
3. is		_____	_____
4. dissected		_____	_____
5. became		_____	_____
6. have disagreed		_____	_____
7. have become heated		_____	_____
8. are visiting		_____	_____
9. has become		_____	_____
10. can purchase		_____	_____

OBSERVATION 3

Directions:

1. Cross out prepositional phrases.

2. Underline the subject once and the verb twice.

Example:

There <u>may be</u> a <u>fragment</u> ~~in my essay~~.

1. The two political parties have disagreed with each other about every issue.

2. The debates have become heated.

3. Sam and Joe are visiting their relatives in Hawaii.

4. For many people, Hawaii has become a popular vacation destination.

5. In the college bookstore, students can purchase books and clothes.

OBSERVATION 4

Directions:

1. In the paragraph below, cross out the prepositional phrases.

2. Beginning with the last sentence and working up to the first one, underline the subject once and the verb twice.

Example:

There <u>may be</u> a <u>fragment</u> ~~in my essay~~.

Every complete sentence contains five elements. At the beginning of the sentence, the first letter is capitalized. A subject and a verb are found somewhere within the sentence. The sentence itself must express a complete thought. Finally, at the end of the sentence, there is a period.

Because a verb shows that the subject exists or is doing something, every sentence must have both a subject and a verb. When you come across a group of words disguised as a sentence but missing either a subject or a verb, it is a fragment and needs to be changed into a complete sentence.

Fragment: ~~For example~~, paragraphs and essays.

With the prepositional phrase crossed out in the above example, you can readily see that there are two subjects: *paragraphs* and *essays*. However, there is no verb showing the reader that the subjects exist or are doing something. To correct this type of fragment, add a verb and any other words necessary to create a complete thought.

Correct: For example, <u>paragraphs</u> and <u>essays</u> <u>need</u> a main idea.

PREPARATION 1

Directions:

1. In each of the fragments below, cross out the prepositional phrases.

2. Add a verb to show that the subject exists or is doing something, and add any other words necessary to complete the sentence.

Examples:

Everyone ~~in the writing class~~ *is here.*

Everyone ~~in this writing class~~ *proofreads carefully.*

1. One of the best resources in the community.

2. Places like the Learning Assistance Center.

3. Anyone in any class on this campus.

4. For instance, the new students on the campus.

5. Most of the students in writing classes.

Always keep in mind that a verb can be either a single word or a verb phrase. Whenever you see a verb ending in ***ing***, look for other verbs in front of it. Because it is not strong enough by itself, an ***ing*** verb has to be part of a verb phrase.

Fragment: Students searching for careers in the medical field.

After crossing out the prepositional phrases, only two words remain.

Fragment: Students searching ~~for careers in the medical field~~.

Obviously, the word *students* is the subject, but the example is still a fragment. *Searching* is an ***ing*** word that needs more verbs with it.

Correct: Students **have been searching** for careers in the medical field.

Correct: Students **will be searching** for careers in the medical field.

Another way to correct this type of fragment is to change the ***ing*** word into a strong verb.

Correct: Students **search** for careers in the medical field.

PREPARATION 2

1. Cross out the prepositional phrases.

2. Correct all of the fragments two ways:

    (1) change the ***ing*** word into a verb phrase

    (2) change the ***ing*** word into a strong verb

Example:

~~To proofread~~, a student isolating sentences ~~from the paragraph~~.

(1) To proofread, a student will be isolating sentences from the paragraph.

(2) To proofread, a student isolates sentences from the paragraph.

1. Students needing assistance with difficult math problems.

    (1)

    (2)

2. A group of pre-school children chasing each other through the yard.

    (1)

    (2)

3. By the light of the moon, the wolves howling.

    (1)

    (2)

4. In front of a large group of family and friends, the couple sealing their vows with a kiss.

    (1)

    (2)

5. The young lady texting on her cell phone for hours and hours.

    (1)

    (2)

PREPARATION 3

Directions:

1. Cross out all prepositional phrases.

2. Starting with the last sentence and ending with the first one, underline the subject (who or what the sentence is about) once and underline the verb (which shows that the subject exists or is doing something) twice.

3. If there is no verb or only a partial verb (***ing*** word), add a helping verb and any other words needed to change the fragment into a complete thought.

Students deciding upon a career field. Medicine, education, or technology. Nursing a popular choice. Another popular career choice is criminal justice. Of all careers, those in engineering have the greatest demand. Therefore, students considering engineering.

ADDING A COMPLETE THOUGHT

Another essential element of every sentence is a complete thought. A group of words may have both a subject and a verb, but if it does not make complete sense by itself, it is still a fragment. Fragments that have a subject and a verb yet lack a complete thought typically begin with a word called a subordinating conjunction.

There are several subordinating conjunctions, but an easy way to remember them is to think of a subway sandwich or a subway train. Now change the *y* to an *i* and you have SUBWAI. SUBWAI stands for the first letters of each of the subordinating conjunctions.

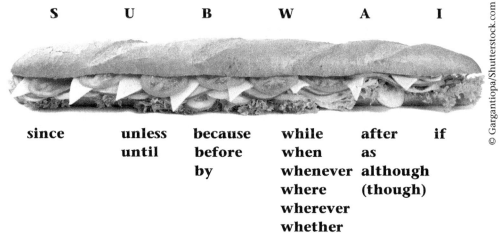

S	U	B	W	A	I
since	unless until	because before by	while when whenever where wherever whether	after as although (though)	if

© Gargantiopa/Shutterstock.com

Here are two examples of SUBWAI fragments:

1. Because the paper was due in the morning.

2. Although research indicates that the medical field is growing.

In the first fragment, the subject is *paper* and the verb is *was due*. However, the SUBWAI word *because* makes the thought incomplete. In the second fragment, the subject is *research* and the verb is *indicates*. Again, however, the SUBWAI word *although* makes the thought incomplete. To eliminate this type of fragment, a complete thought must be placed either before or after the incomplete thought.

OBSERVATION 1

Directions:

1. Circle the SUBWAI word in each word group.

2. If the thought is incomplete, write the number 0 in the blank.

3. If the thought is complete, write the number 1 in the blank and underline the words that are a complete thought.

Examples:

 _0_ (Whenever) a student writes a paper.

 _1_ (Whenever) a student writes a paper, <u>she learns how to express her ideas.</u>

___ 1. If a sentence does not contain a complete thought.

___ 2. After staying up late last night to proofread his paper.

___ 3. After staying up late last night, he fell asleep in class this morning.

___ 4. It is not a true sentence if it does not contain a complete thought.

___ 5. When a person is physically exhausted.

___ 6. He fell asleep in class this morning because he stayed up late last night.

___ 7. Since proofreading requires being mentally and physically alert.

___ 8. A person can fall asleep anywhere when he is physically exhausted.

___ 9. Until a person has revised her paper several times.

___10. A person is not ready for proofreading until she has revised her paper several times.

Did you notice that when the SUBWAI word is at the beginning, the complete thought is at the end of the sentence? Conversely, when the SUBWAI word is somewhere in the middle of the sentence, the complete thought is at the beginning.

OBSERVATION 2

Directions:

1. Circle all of the SUBWAI words.

2. Starting with the last sentence that contains a SUBWAI word and working up to the first one, underline the part that makes it a complete thought.

Examples:

(Whenever) a student writes a paper, <u>she learns how to express her ideas</u>.

<u>A student learns how to express her ideas</u> (whenever) she writes a paper.

Although it is a common practice, it is not a good idea to wait until the last minute to proofread. Many people put off proofreading because they think that all they have to do is read the draft one more time. However, proofreading is a time-consuming process when it is done correctly. Unless they do not care about how well they are communicating, writers should set aside a couple of days for the important task of proofreading.

Every sentence must convey a complete thought. When you come across a group of words disguised as a sentence but missing a complete thought, it is a fragment and needs a complete thought added to it. To correct SUBWAI fragments, you can choose from one of the following two options:

Option 1: After the fragment, add a comma and a complete thought.

Incorrect: Because the paper was due in the morning.

Correct: Because the paper was due in the morning, <u>Miguel had to stay up all night</u>.

Option 2: Before the fragment, add a complete thought. No comma is needed with this option.

Incorrect: Because the paper was due in the morning.

Correct: <u>Miguel had to stay up all night</u> because his paper was due in the morning.

PREPARATION 1

After each fragment, add a comma and full sentence.

Directions:

1. Circle the SUBWAI word.

2. After each fragment, add a comma and a full sentence.

Example:

(Although) research indicates that the medical field will grow, *there are other fields that will grow even more quickly.*

1. If a group of words does not contain a complete thought.

2. After staying up late last night to proofread his paper.

3. When a person is physically exhausted.

4. Since proofreading requires being mentally and physically alert.

5. Until a person has revised her paper several times.

PREPARATION 2

1. Circle the SUBWAI word.

2. In the blank line, write a complete sentence first and attach the fragment after it.

Example:

(If) you proofread your paper carefully.
*You will make a higher grade **if** you proofread your paper carefully.*

1. If a group of words does not contain a complete thought.

   _____

   _____

2. After staying up late last night to proofread his paper.

   _____

   _____

3. When he is physically exhausted.

   _____

   _____

4. Since proofreading requires being mentally and physically alert.

   _____

   _____

5. Until Tamekia has revised her paper several times.

   _____

   _____

In the last two practices, you had to add the missing sentences to the fragments. In a paragraph or an essay, the writer may have already written a complete thought that goes with the fragment either immediately before or immediately after it. When that is the case, you simply have to attach the fragment to the complete thought.

PREPARATION 3

Directions:

1. Circle all of the SUBWAI words.

2. Starting with the last SUBWAI word, read the sentence to determine if it is complete or incomplete. If it is complete, go to the next-to-last SUBWAI word.

3. If it is a fragment, determine which sentence should be attached to it.

   (a) If the fragment goes with the sentence before it, put them together with no comma between them.

   (b) If the fragment goes with the sentence after it, put them together with a comma between them.

Although the need for engineers is great. The number of engineers is low. Many people do not major in engineering. Because this field requires mathematical skills. Since the demand for engineers will continue to increase. All students who are good in math should explore the engineering field. When they graduate from college. Jobs will be available to them.

Proofreading to End a Complete Thought

You now know how to find fragments and correct them by adding missing parts: subjects, verbs, and complete thoughts. Now it is time to apply that information to other writers' paragraphs and then to your own writing. While it is not easy to catch fragments buried within paragraphs and essays, following the step-by-step system covered in this section will help you achieve excellent results. To proofread others' writings, work through the following three stages:

1. Isolate the sentences from the paragraph.

2. Analyze each sentence to determine if it is complete or incomplete.

3. Correct the incomplete thoughts by adding the missing part(s).

APPLICATION 1

Directions:

Stage 1:

To isolate the sentences in the paragraph below, take a blank sheet of paper and cover up all the sentences except the last one. Continue isolating all the sentences in the paragraph by uncovering and reading from the last one up to the first one.

Stage 2:

As you read each isolated sentence aloud, say the words ***I realize*** first. If the sentence makes sense with those words added to it, it is a complete thought. If it does not make sense, it is an incomplete thought.

Stage 3:

If it is incomplete, correct it by giving it all five essential parts of a sentence: a capital letter, a subject, a verb, a complete thought, and a period.

The worst job I ever had was working at a fast-food restaurant. Here in town. For one thing, the managers would bring their problems to work and take out their anger on the employees. Barking orders and making us do all the dirty work. Another reason why it was the worst job is that my co-workers did not get along with each other. One time three of them got into an argument about whose turn it was to clean the bathrooms. Because they refused to reach an agreement. They all quit. Leaving me to do the job. When I had been the last person to clean the bathrooms. The final factor that made this job the worst was that I was not rewarded for my good nature, long hours, and hard work. When the managers interviewed me for the job. They said my starting salary would be $7.00 an hour and that I would get a quarter raise every three months. Twelve months later, I was still making $7.00 an hour. Finally, having had enough of angry managers, argumentative co-workers, and no promotions. I left the worst job ever.

APPLICATION 2

Directions:

Stage 1:

To isolate the sentences in the paragraph below, take a blank sheet of paper and cover up all the sentences except the last one. Continue isolating all the sentences in the paragraph by uncovering and reading from the last one up to the first one.

Stage 2:

As you read each isolated sentence aloud, say the words **_I realize_** first. If the sentence makes sense with those words added to it, it is a complete thought. If it does not make sense, it is an incomplete thought.

Stage 3:

If it is incomplete, correct it by giving it all five essential parts of a sent€ capital letter, a subject, a verb, a complete thought, and a period.

It may seem hard to believe, but the best job I ever had was working at a small fast-food restaurant. The owner, Ms. Goodman, made the job a great one. First, she personally interviewed, hired, and trained every employee. Used humor to teach us how to make the food. Encouraged us as we were learning. Secondly, Ms. Goodman worked at the restaurant several days a week. Leading by example. She always had a smile on her face. And made every customer feel welcomed. Finally, she made her employees feel they were valuable and rewarded them with raises. One night I filled in for a sick employee after working my regular shift. Afterwards Ms. Goodman thanked me, told me I was doing a great job, and increased my pay. An extra dollar an hour. If I had not moved to another town. I would still be working there. Because it was the best job I have ever had.

APPLICATION 3

Finally, it is time for you to apply all of the information you have learned in this chapter to proofread your own paper. For your final draft, you will follow a four-stage proofreading process that will take about fifteen minutes per paragraph. The results will be well worth the time and effort.

Stage One: Isolating Your Sentences

To isolate the sentences in your own writing, follow these four steps:

Step 1: On a computer, open the final draft of your paper.

Step 2: Go to the beginning of the last paragraph and click on the numbering icon. The number 1 will appear in front of your paragraph. The following example illustrates where the icon and the number appear in Microsoft Word.

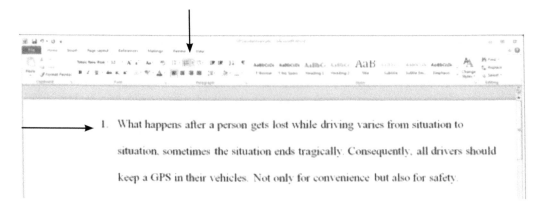

Step 3: Press the enter key after every period in the paragraph. This action will convert your paragraph into a list of individually numbered sentences. The following example illustrates how this looks in Microsoft Word.

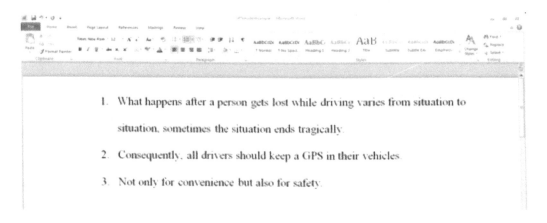

Step 4: Print out only the page that contains your isolated sentences.

To analyze each sentence of your paper, follow these three steps:

Step 1: Look at the last isolated sentence on your printed page. Slowly read it aloud, adding the words *I realize* to the beginning of the sentence. This technique will help you hear if you have omitted any words or have written something that does not make sense by itself.

Step 2: Ask, "Is this a full sentence? Does it make complete sense all by itself?" Do **not** look at the sentence before it. If you cannot keep from peeking, then cover up the previous sentences with a sheet of paper. The sentence you are focusing on has to be able to stand alone without using the rest of the paragraph as a crutch. If it does not make sense by itself, write a zero in front of it.

O 4. Not only for convenience but also for safety.

Step 3: Repeat the above two steps with the next-to-last sentence. Continue repeating the same two steps, analyzing each isolated sentence in reverse order until you end up at your first sentence last.

Stage Three: Correcting Your Sentences

In this chapter, there is only one step at this stage:

Step 1: Correct all incomplete sentences with a zero written in front of them. They are fragments that must be turned into sentences by adding whatever parts are missing: subject, verb, complete thought.

Stage Four: Returning Your Sentences to Paragraph Form for the Final Polish

To return your sentences to paragraph form, follow these two steps:

Step 1: Place your cursor in front of the last sentence and hit the backspace key as many times as needed until it is one space after the previous period. Repeat with each sentence. This action deletes the numbers. The following example illustrates how this looks in Microsoft Word.

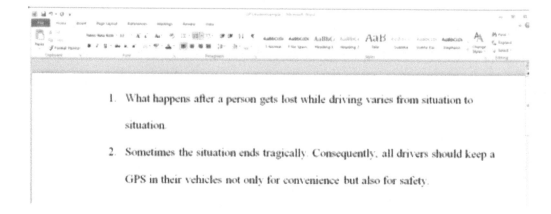

1. What happens after a person gets lost while driving varies from situation to situation.

2. Sometimes the situation ends tragically. Consequently, all drivers should keep a GPS in their vehicles not only for convenience but also for safety.

Step 2: Backspace your first sentence until it reaches the left margin. Next, press the tab key one time. Your sentences are now back together as a properly indented paragraph. Be sure to save your work.

If your instructor assigned a multi-paragraph essay, you will repeat all four stages of the proofreading process (isolating, analyzing, correcting, and returning) with every paragraph in your essay. Since you have already proofread your last paragraph, you are now ready to proofread your next-to-last paragraph. Continue proofreading in reverse order until you finish your first paragraph last. Be sure to save your work after proofreading each paragraph.

Polishing the Final Draft

After you have completed all four stages of the proofreading process for each paragraph, print out your final draft. Slowly read it aloud from beginning to end to make sure that you actually made all the changes you intended to make. You may find it even more helpful to get a friend to read it aloud slowly while you listen. Your friend will read it exactly the way it appears on the paper rather than the way you think you wrote it, thus making it easier for you to catch any further errors. This is your last chance to turn your paper into a polished final draft deserving of a high grade, so allow yourself enough time to do a thorough proofreading job.

CHAPTER 2

Separating Two Complete Thoughts

In this chapter, you will learn how to proofread your papers to clearly separate sentences from each other. After you have successfully completed this chapter, you should be able to do the following:

- Recognize a run-on sentence.
- Distinguish between the two types of run-on sentences.
- Recall and apply three punctuation options to clearly separate sentences.
- Analyze writings to determine if incomplete or run-on sentences exist.
- Apply proofreading techniques to make sentences complete and clearly separated.

Identifying Two Types of Run-on Sentences

As a child, you learned that the primary purpose for punctuation is to end a complete sentence. You also learned that by doing so, you simultaneously separate each sentence from the next one. Surprisingly though, the most common writing error that college students make is the incorrect separation of two sentences.

When proper punctuation is not placed between two complete thoughts, the sentences run into each other. This type of error is called a run-on sentence and is the equivalent of a wreck between two cars.

A run-on forces your readers to back up and try to determine for themselves where the first sentence should have ended. Readers do not like trying to read your mind. English instructors find run-ons particularly annoying and take off several points each time a student's paper makes them back-track. Consequently, you want to avoid run-on sentences at all costs in your final draft.

Before proofreading your essay to see if it has any run-on sentences, you will first need to learn how to identify them. There are two types of run-on sentences, and both mistakes are equally serious:

1. Fused sentences

2. Comma splices

IDENTIFYING FUSED SENTENCES

When two sentences run into each other with no punctuation mark between them, they join together incorrectly as one sentence. This type of run-on is called a fused

sentence. Although you can fuse two wires together to make them into one, you cannot fuse two sentences together.

OBSERVATION 1

All of the sentences below are incorrectly fused together.

Directions:

1. Underline the first sentence in red. Underline the second sentence in blue.

2. Draw a circle at the spot where the two sentences run into each other.

Example:

This is one complete sentence◯ it is followed by another complete sentence.

1. Janetta wrote a descriptive paper in one day she revised it in fourteen days.

2. She sent John an email he replied immediately.

3. Sentences that focus on one point form a paragraph several paragraphs that focus on one main idea form an essay.

4. Writing is easy revising is hard.

5. Students should revise their papers a few times then they will be ready to proofread for errors.

OBSERVATION 2

Some of the sentences below are correct while others are fused sentences.

Directions:

1. Underline the first sentence in red, and underline the second sentence in blue.

2. If the sentences are incorrectly fused together, draw a circle at the spot where they run into each other. If correct, leave as is.

Examples:

This is one complete sentence◯it is followed by another complete sentence.

This is one complete sentence. It is followed by another complete sentence.

1. Writing is more involved than simply producing a single draft it takes a lot of time and effort.

2. A first draft requires inspiration. A revised draft requires perspiration.

3. A final draft requires dedication this makes the difference between an average paper and a great one.

4. Because revising is a lengthy process, it is best to work on the assignment a few minutes each day then the task does not become impossible.

5. Writing only one or two drafts may be easier. However, writing several drafts will result in a better paper.

IDENTIFYING COMMA SPLICES

Some people mistaken-ly believe that putting a comma between two sentences will solve the problem of a run-on. However, a comma is much too weak to do the job of a period. A comma cannot separate two complete sentences any more effectively than a person can separate two angry elephants.

© eelnosiva/Shutterstock.com

If you do make the mistake of putting a comma between two sentences, you still have a run-on. This type of run-on is called a comma splice because the two sentences are spliced together with a weak comma.

OBSERVATION 3

Each of the sentences below is a comma splice.

Directions:

1. Underline the first sentence in red, and underline the second sentence in blue.

2. Draw a circle around the comma that incorrectly splices the two sentences.

Example:

This is one complete sentence, it is followed by another complete sentence.

1. Writing is easy, revising is hard.

2. Systematic proofreading is easy, it just takes some time to do it well.

3. Each sentence must be isolated from the rest of the paragraph, then the writer can analyze it for errors.

4. Understanding the purposes for punctuation helps writers find and correct errors, this knowledge increases their confidence in their proofreading abilities.

5. After identifying incomplete and run-on sentences, the writer turns them into complete and clearly separated sentences, then she puts them back into the paragraph.

OBSERVATION 4

Some of the sentences below are two sentences punctuated correctly while others are comma splices.

Directions:

1. Underline the first sentence in red. Underline the second sentence in blue.

2. If the sentences are incorrectly spliced together, draw a circle around the comma that runs them into each other. If correct, leave as is.

Examples:

This is one complete sentence, it is followed by another complete sentence.

This is one complete sentence. It is followed by another complete sentence.

1. Writing is more involved than simply producing a single draft, it takes a lot of time and effort.

2. A first draft requires inspiration, a revised draft requires perspiration.

3. A final draft requires dedication. This makes the difference between an average paper and a great one.

4. Because writing is a lengthy process, it is best to work on the assignment each day, then the task does not become impossible.

5. Writing only one draft may be easier, however, writing several drafts results in a better paper.

Correcting Run-on Sentences

As a student, you want to avoid both types of run-on sentences (fused sentences and comma splices) on your final draft so that you can make a good grade. As a writer, you need to separate your sentences correctly so that your readers understand exactly where each complete thought ends. Both types of run-on sentences can be corrected in any of the following three ways:

Option #1: Put a period between the two sentences.

Option #2: Put a semicolon between the two sentences.

Option #3: Put a comma before a coordinating conjunction between the two sentences.

Each time you reach the end of a sentence that you have written, you get to choose which option you want to use. Let's now consider each of your choices.

SEPARATING SENTENCES WITH A PERIOD

The first option for correcting a run-on sentence is the most common: put a period between the two sentences. As you know, this tiny dot is the strongest punctuation mark in the English language. (Actually, the exclamation point is the strongest mark but is used in academic writing only when quoting someone who is yelling.) Although Americans call the dot a period, the British have a better term for it: a full stop.

© PanicAttack/Shutterstock.com

Example: A GPS dictates every step. It leads the driver to his destination.

Example: This sentence is short. Then it is followed by a slightly longer sentence.

OBSERVATION 1

Directions:

1. Underline the first sentence in red. Underline the second sentence in blue.

2. Circle the period that indicates separation between two sentences.

Example:

This exercise is easy. The next one is also easy.

1. A few changes can make a small closet seem larger. They also make the space more functional.

2. The most obvious change starts with de-cluttering. All items that have not been worn in the past two years should be sold or given away.

3. Home improvement stores carry a variety of closet organizing systems that fit small closets. Many of these systems are portable and set up in a few minutes.

4. Although it sounds frivolous, buying velvet hangers for every hanging item frees up a lot of closet space. Their thin profile and grip on clothing also make a small closet look neater and cleaner.

5. One final change that makes a small closet seem larger is grouping the clothing by color. Although this tip does not actually enlarge the space, it effectively fools the eye into believing the space is larger.

PREPARATION 1

Directions:

1. Underline the first sentence in red. Underline the second sentence in blue.

2. Put a period and a capital letter between the two sentences.

Example:

T
This exercise is easy. the next one is also easy.

1. Americans call the dot at the end of a sentence a period the British call it a full stop.

2. A period ends a complete sentence at the same time, it separates one sentence from the next.

3. Both a statement and an indirect question end with a period, a direct question ends with a question mark.

4. Americans call the dot at the end of a sentence a period, the British call it a full stop.

5. A period ends a complete sentence, at the same time, it separates one sentence from the next.

PREPARATION 2

Directions:

1. Read the last sentence first. If it is only one sentence, it is correct.

2. If two sentences are fused together, correct them by putting a period and a capital letter between them.

3. Proceed in reverse order through the rest of the paragraph.

The lake does not look like a picture it is picture-perfect. No rays of sunlight dance on the water the clouds cover the sky and prevent the sun's rays from stretching down to the lake. No breeze blows no waves ripple on the water's surface. The lake is calm and beautiful.

PREPARATION 3

Directions:

1. Circle all the commas in the paragraph below.

2. Beginning with the last comma in the paragraph, first read the words after the comma and then read the words before the comma.

3. If one side of the comma is a sentence but the other side is not, it is correct.

4. If there are two sentences (one on each side of the comma), it is incorrect. Change the inadequate comma to a period and capitalize the second sentence.

5. Proceed in reverse order through the rest of the paragraph.

The lake does not look like a picture, it is picture-perfect. No rays of sunlight dance on the water, the clouds cover the sky and prevent the sun's rays from stretching down to the lake. No breeze blows, no waves ripple on the water's surface. The lake is calm and beautiful.

SEPARATING SENTENCES WITH A SEMICOLON

Another way to prevent a run-on is to put a semicolon between the two sentences. A semicolon means basically the same thing as a period and is equivalent to a "California stop." You don't make a full stop; instead, you slow down and roll almost to a stop but then keep on going. Although a "California stop" is illegal when driving, you are allowed to use a semicolon instead of a period when writing to show readers that the two sentences are closely related in thought.

Example: A GPS dictates every step; it leads the driver to her destination.

Example: This sentence is short; then it is followed by a slightly longer sentence.

OBSERVATION 1

Directions:

1. Underline the first sentence in red; underline the second sentence in blue.

2. Circle the semicolon that separates the two sentences.

Example:

This exercise is easy; the next one is also easy.

1. A period separates two sentences; a semicolon separates two related sentences.

2. One way to prevent a run-on is to separate two sentences with a period; another way is to use a semicolon.

3. Janetta wrote her first draft in one day; then she revised it several times over a two-week period.

4. Writing is easy; revising is hard.

5. Isolating sentences from the paragraph is the first stage of proofreading; it helps the writer focus on one sentence at a time.

OBSERVATION 2

Some of the sentences below are two sentences combined correctly while others are only one long sentence.

Directions:

1. In the blank line, write a 1 if it is only one sentence.

2. In the blank line, write a 2 if it is two combined sentences. Underline the first sentence in red, and underline the second sentence in blue.

Examples:

_1_ Although this sentence may look like two combined sentences, it is actually only one long sentence.

_2_ This sentence may look like only one sentence; it is actually two combined sentences.

___1. When the sky turns dark, it is time to take cover.

___2. The sky turned dark; everyone ran for shelter.

___3. If a subordinating conjunction starts a sentence, that sentence will have an incomplete thought followed by a complete thought.

___4. A sentence must make complete sense by itself; a fragment does not make sense by itself.

___5. After looking at a sentence carefully, a person can determine if it contains one or two complete thoughts.

PREPARATION 1

All of the sentences below contain both types of run-ons: fused sentences and comma splices.

Directions:

1. Underline the first sentence in red; underline the second sentence in blue.

2. Put a semicolon between the two sentences.

Example:

This exercise is easy; the next one is also easy.

1. Americans call the dot at the end of a sentence a period the British call it a full stop.

2. A period ends a complete sentence at the same time, it separates one sentence from the next.

3. Both a statement and an indirect question end with a period, a direct question ends with a question mark.

4. Americans call the dot at the end of a sentence a period, the British call it a full stop.

5. A period ends a complete sentence, at the same time, it separates one sentence from the next.

ADDING TRANSITIONS BETWEEN SENTENCES

You may wish to add a transition word or phrase (extra information) between the two sentences, as in the following examples.

Example: A GPS dictates every step; ultimately, it leads the driver to her destination.

Example: The student carefully followed the four stages of proofreading; of course, he earned a high grade on his essay.

Notice that you still place a semicolon between the two sentences; furthermore, you add a comma after the transition to show that it is extra information before the second sentence begins. You will learn more about separating extra information from the sentence itself in Chapter 4.

OBSERVATION 3

Directions:

1. Underline the first sentence in red; underline the second sentence in blue.

2. Circle the semicolon that separates the two sentences.

3. Draw a square around the comma that separates the transition from the second sentence.

Example:

This exercise is easy; moreover, the next one is also easy.

1. The period is like a full stop; consequently, it is needed after a complete sentence.

2. A period typically goes between two sentences; however, it is not the only way to separate sentences.

3. The semicolon also separates two complete sentences; furthermore, it indicates that the two sentences are closely related in thought.

4. The period makes a full stop at the end of a sentence; on the other hand, a semicolon is like a "California stop."

5. A "California stop" is not a full stop; instead, the driver rolls almost to a stop but keeps on going.

PREPARATION 2

Directions:

1. Underline the first sentence in red; underline the second sentence in blue.

2. Put a semicolon between the two sentences.

3. Put a comma after the transition (extra information) at the start of the second sentence.

Example:

This exercise is easy; moreover, the next one is also easy.

1. People use their cell phones for socializing in addition they use them for surfing the internet.

2. Many young people prefer to text rather than talk on the phone therefore they should purchase unlimited text-messaging plans.

3. Smart phones are expensive nevertheless many people buy them.

4. They want a cell phone that can do everything of course no phone is perfect.

5. Buyers must also choose a monthly plan that is compatible with their phone moreover they must pay for that plan every month.

PREPARATION 3

Directions:

1. Read the last sentence first. If it is only one sentence, it is correct.

2. If it is a fused sentence, correct it by putting either a period or a semicolon between the two sentences.

3. Proceed in reverse order through the rest of the paragraph.

Cats make better pets than dogs. For starters, cats are easier to housebreak their owners have to show them where the litter box is only one time. Dogs take weeks to train many leave puddles and messes around the house their entire lives. Cats groom themselves dogs cannot clean themselves. Finally, cats are loving when their owners have time to cuddle them but self-sufficient when their owners are busy.

PREPARATION 4

Directions:

1. Circle all commas in the following paragraph.

2. Beginning with the last comma in the paragraph, first read the words after the comma and then read the words before the comma.

3. If one side of the comma is a sentence but the other side is not, it is correct.

4. If there are two sentences (one on each side of the comma), it is incorrect. Change the comma to either a semicolon or a period.

5. Proceed in reverse order through the rest of the paragraph.

Dogs make better pets than cats. When their owners come home after a long day of work, dogs run and greet them happily, cats keep their distance and act disinterested. Dogs enjoy every activity their owners enjoy. Whether it is jogging or eating, it does not matter. All that matters to dogs is that they are fed and cared for by their owners, then their dogs reward them with loyalty.

OBSERVATION 4

Directions:

1. Underline the first sentence in red; underline the second sentence in blue.

2. Circle the punctuation mark that indicates separation between two sentences.

3. Circle which option was used to separate the sentences.

Example:

This exercise is easy; the next one is also easy.

Period   Semicolon

1. Both a statement and an indirect question end with a period. A direct question ends with a question mark.

Period   Semicolon

2. The semicolon also separates two complete sentences; furthermore, it indicates that the two sentences are closely related in thought.

Period   Semicolon

3. Writing is easy. Revising is hard work.

Period   Semicolon

4. Proofreading is easy; however, it is time-consuming.

Period   Semicolon

5. Writing is easy; revising is hard work.

Period   Semicolon

SEPARATING SENTENCES WITH A COMMA BEFORE FANBOYS

The third way to prevent a run-on is to put a comma **plus** one of these seven words between the two sentences: for, and, nor, but, or, yet, so. This rule works **only** with these seven words (called coordinating conjunctions) and no others. An easy way to remember them is to think of the word FANBOYS.

© robbylokamp/Shutterstock.com

F = for   B = but

A = and   O = or

N = nor   Y = yet

                S = so

Example: A GPS dictates every step, **and** it leads you to your destination.

Example: This first sentence is short, **but** the second sentence is longer and appears after a coordinating conjunction.

Example: John was not awake, **so** Mary ate his breakfast.

This option for connecting two sentences is like a yield sign. Although you slow down, you keep on going.

© Handies Peak/Shutterstock.com

Coordinating conjunctions (FANBOYS) tell readers the connection between the two sentences; therefore, the writer must choose the correct FANBOYS word. As Mark Twain once said, "The difference between the right word and the almost right word is the difference between lightning and the lightning bug."

For = The second sentence is the reason behind the first sentence. "For" has the same meaning as the word "because."

Example: Japan is raising the price of its vehicles in the American market, for the yen has lost value next to the dollar.

And = The second sentence adds to the first sentence.

Example: Toyota and Honda are two well-known automobile manufacturers, and their vehicles are quite popular in the United States.

Nor = Both sentences are negative statements.

Example: Toyota does not have an all-electric vehicle in the United States, nor does Honda have an all-electric vehicle at this time.

But = The second sentence is in contrast to the first sentence.

Example: Toyota does not have an all-electric vehicle in the United States, but Honda will have one on the market soon.

Or = The two sentences explain two options or choices.

Example: Toyota needs to produce an all-electric vehicle for the United States, or it will lose its first-place standing in the market.

Yet = The second sentence is true, too, despite the truth of the first sentence.

Example: Young children learn to separate two sentences with a period, yet many adults do not separate sentences properly.

So = The second sentence is a result of the first sentence.

Example: Some college students do not separate sentences properly, so their writing instructors need to review the three ways to separate sentences.

OBSERVATION 1

Directions:

1. Underline the first sentence in red, and underline the second sentence in blue.

2. Circle the comma and coordinating conjunction (FANBOYS) that separates the two sentences.

Example:

This exercise is easy, (and) the next one is also easy.

1. Writing is easy, but revising is hard work.

2. Writing is a lengthy process, yet it is also rewarding.

3. Maria goes to school three days a week, and she goes to work on the other days of the week.

4. She likes to stay in touch with her friends, so she has an unlimited text-messaging plan.

5. Yvette needs to spend more time revising her paper, or she will not earn a high grade.

PREPARATION 1

Directions:

1. Underline the first sentence in red, and underline the second sentence in blue.

2. If missing, insert a comma plus a coordinating conjunction (FANBOYS) between the two sentences.

Examples:

and
<u>This exercise is easy</u>, the next one is also easy.
^

, and
<u>This exercise is easy</u> the next one is also easy.
^

1. Eye surgery can correct vision problems it cannot reverse the aging process.

2. The movie was released last year, the sequel came out this year.

3. A blizzard is headed for this area people are stocking up on food.

4. Umbrellas sell out quickly at amusement parks, visitors are unprepared for sudden rain showers.

5. Students learn the main purpose for punctuation in grade school, they struggle with punctuation rules in college.

When using this third method for correcting run-ons, remember that you cannot put only a comma between two sentences. It is absolutely crucial that you put a coordinating conjunction after the comma. However, do not let that reminder cause you to overuse commas and place them in front of every coordinating conjunction you see. If you are in doubt as to whether or not you need a comma, draw a box around the FANBOYS word in question. Then read the words after the FANBOYS word. Do they make up a complete sentence? If so, read the words before the FANBOYS word. Do they make up another complete sentence? If you have a complete sentence on both sides of the FANBOYS word, then you must put a comma before it. However, if one side of the FANBOYS word is a sentence but the other side is not, you do not need a comma.

Example: A complete sentence is before the coordinating conjunction, and another complete sentence is after the coordinating conjunction.

Example: There is a complete sentence before the coordinating conjunction but not after it.

OBSERVATION 3

1. Draw a box around each FANBOYS word.

2. If there is no comma in front of the FANBOYS word, it is only one sentence and should not be underlined.

3. If there is a comma in front of the FANBOYS word, underline the sentence before it in red and the sentence after it in blue.

Examples:

There is a complete sentence before the coordinating conjunction but not after it.

A complete sentence is before the coordinating conjunction, and another complete sentence is after the coordinating conjunction.

1. It is easy to write when the topic is inspiring, but it is difficult when the topic is boring.

2. The writer must revise his paper thoroughly, or his readers will not understand him clearly.

3. Writing is easy, yet revising is hard work.

4. It is easy to write when the topic is inspiring and exciting.

5. The writer must revise her paper thoroughly, for her readers cannot read her mind.

PREPARATION 2

Directions:

1. Circle every FANBOYS word in the sentences below.

2. If one side of the FANBOYS word is a sentence but the other side is not, it is correct.

3. If there is a complete sentence on both sides of the FANBOYS word, insert a comma.

Example:

This exercise is easy, and the next one is also easy but longer.

1. New cars depreciate quickly so buying a used car is a wiser investment.

2. You can separate two sentences with a period or with a comma.

3. You can also separate two sentences with a comma and a coordinating conjunction.

4. Many people like the idea of driving an all-electric car but are concerned about the low mileage range.

5 Many people like the idea of driving an all-electric car but they are concerned about the low mileage range.

PREPARATION 3

Directions:

1. Read the last sentence first. If it is only one sentence, it is correct.

2. If it is two sentences fused together, correct it. Use each option (period, semicolon, comma before coordinating conjunction) at least one time.

3. Proceed in reverse order through the rest of the paragraph.

The city park provides visitors with opportunities for recreation it also provides opportunities for relaxation. People can play tennis on the courts or swim in the Olympic-sized pool they can hike on the trails or bike on the roads. Numerous benches are placed throughout the park they can take a break from their activities. They can also eat a picnic lunch under one of the many pavilions.

PREPARATION 4

Directions:

1. Circle all the commas in the following paragraph.

2. Starting with the last comma, first read the words after it and then read the words before it.

3. If one side of the comma is a sentence but the other side is not, it is correct.

4. If there are two sentences (one on each side of the comma), it is incorrect. Use each option for correcting run-on sentences (period, semicolon, comma before coordinating conjunction) at least one time.

5. Proceed in reverse order through the rest of the paragraph.

Students and professors alike have mixed opinions about on-line courses. Some people like them, others avoid them. For people with schedules that vary from week to week, on-line courses give them instant access at their convenience. They can work at their own pace, it does require a healthy amount of self-discipline. For those people who do not have excellent computer skills and self-discipline, on-line courses are difficult, they become too challenging too quickly. Although not everyone shares the same opinion about these courses, it is nice to have options.

OBSERVATION 2

Directions:

1. Underline the first sentence in red, and underline the second sentence in blue.

2. Circle the area that indicates separation between the two sentences.

3. Circle which option was used to separate them.

Example:

This exercise is easy, (and) the next one is also easy.

    Period   Semicolon   (Comma before FANBOYS)

1. A period separates two sentences. A semicolon also separates two sentences.

    Period   Semicolon   Comma before FANBOYS

2. A period typically separates two sentences, but a comma and a coordinating conjunction can also separate them.

    Period   Semicolon   Comma before FANBOYS

3. Coordinating conjunctions show the relationship between two sentences, so it is important to choose the correct conjunction.

    Period   Semicolon   Comma before FANBOYS

4. The semicolon separates two sentences; moreover, it indicates that they are closely related in thought.

    Period   Semicolon   Comma before FANBOYS

5. There are three methods for correcting run-on sentences. The writer gets to choose which method is best to use for each sentence.

    Period   Semicolon   Comma before FANBOYS

APPLICATION 1

The following paragraph has both types of run-ons: two fused sentences and two comma splices.

1. Read the last sentence first. If it is only one sentence, it is correct.

2. If it is a run-on, correct it. Use each option (period, semicolon, comma before coordinating conjunction) at least one time.

3. Proceed in reverse order through the rest of the paragraph.

Vivid colors and superior graphic details initially attract gamers to a particular video game, the variables are what hold their attention. While the element of surprise keeps a game interesting, other variables must also exist. Two of the more common ones are the frequency and speed of attacks other variables are levels of immunity and the number of ways to obtain it. The ability to increase skill is important, it is also fun to be rewarded when taking risks. One final but important variable is the level of accuracy it can make or break the thrill of the game. When all of the variables are present in one game, they can keep the players occupied for hours.

In the previous chapter, you learned how to find and correct fragments (incomplete sentences). In this chapter, you have learned how to find and correct the opposite problem: two complete sentences run together. Now it is time to combine that knowledge and apply it to other writers' paragraphs and then to your own writing. To proofread others' writings, work through the following three stages:

1. Isolate the sentences from the paragraph.

2. Analyze each sentence to determine if it is an incomplete thought or two complete thoughts run together.

3. Correct the thoughts that are incomplete and the sentences that are run together.

APPLICATION 2

Directions:

Stage 1:

Take a blank sheet of paper and cover up all the sentences in the paragraph below except the last one. Continue isolating all the sentences in the paragraph by uncovering and reading from the last one up to the first one.

Stage 2:

As you read each isolated sentence aloud, ask if it is an incomplete thought or two sentences run together.

Stage 3:

If it is an incomplete thought, change it from a fragment into a complete sentence. You may wish to review Chapter 1. If it is two sentences run together, correct it by clearly separating the sentences with a period, a semicolon, or a comma before a FANBOYS word.

When students first enroll in college. They are issued an e-mail school address. E-mail is the primary method that the college uses for communicating important matters such as financial aid and course changes, therefore, students need to read and attend to their e-mail account four to five days a week. The number of e-mails quickly piles up and can clog an account, then students miss crucial deadlines. Students have to remember to delete each e-mail after they have attended to it then it goes into a folder. About once a week, students should delete everything in that folder this action keeps e-mail accounts functioning smoothly.

APPLICATION 3

Directions:

Stage 1:

Take a blank sheet of paper and cover up all the sentences in the paragraph below except the last one. Continue isolating all the sentences in the paragraph by uncovering and reading from the last one up to the first one.

Stage 2:

As you read each isolated sentence aloud, ask if it is an incomplete thought or two sentences run together.

Stage 3:

If it is an incomplete thought, change it from a fragment into a complete sentence. You may wish to review Chapter 1. If it is two sentences run together, correct it by clearly separating the sentences with a period, a semicolon, or a comma before a FANBOYS word.

Michael has difficulty in his English class. He does not have anyone who can help him with his homework. Also, there are no computers in his classroom he has to rush around campus trying to find a computer to use. Fortunately, the college Michael attends now offering a new type of class called Triple-T English. The first T stands for tutor-integrated, the second T stands for technology-embedded. The third T stands for time-on-task, this means students have an extra hour per class period to work on assignments. There are many students like Michael who need extra help in English they should consider enrolling in Triple-T classes.

APPLICATION 4

Finally, it is time for you to apply all of the information you have learned in this chapter and the previous one to proofread your own paper. For your final draft, you will follow a four-stage proofreading process that will take about fifteen minutes per paragraph. The results will be well worth the time and effort.

Stage One: Isolating Your Sentences

To isolate the sentences in your own writing, follow these four steps:

Step 1: On a computer, open the final draft of your paper.

Step 2: Go to the beginning of the last paragraph and click on the numbering icon. The number 1 will appear in front of your paragraph. The following example illustrates where the icon and the number appear in Microsoft Word.

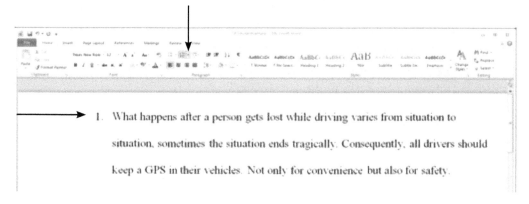

Step 3: Press the enter key after every period in the paragraph. This action will convert your paragraph into a list of individually numbered sentences. The following example illustrates how this looks in Microsoft Word.

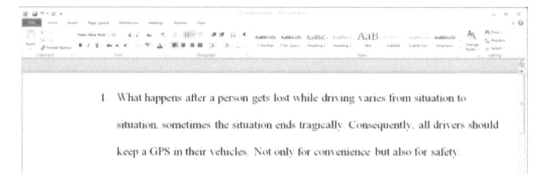

1. What happens after a person gets lost while driving varies from situation to situation, sometimes the situation ends tragically. Consequently, all drivers should keep a GPS in their vehicles. Not only for convenience but also for safety.

Step 4: Print out only the page that contains your isolated sentences.

Stage Two: Analyzing Your Sentences

To analyze each sentence of your paper, follow these four steps:

Step 1: Look at the last isolated sentence on your printed page. **Slowly** read it aloud, adding the words *I realize* to the beginning of the sentence. This technique will help you hear if you have omitted any words or have written something that does not make sense by itself.

Step 2: Ask, "Is this a full sentence? Does it make complete sense all by itself?" Do **not** look at the sentence before it. If you cannot keep from peeking, then cover up the previous sentences with a sheet of paper. The sentence you are focusing on has to make sense without using the rest of the paragraph as a crutch. If it does not make sense by itself, write a zero in front of it.

> *0*   4. Not only for convenience but also for safety.

Step 3: If the sentence does make sense by itself, then ask, "Is it two complete thoughts crammed together?" If so, write a two in front of it.

> *2*   1. What happens after a person gets lost while driving varies from situation to situation, sometimes the situation ends tragically.

Step 4: Repeat the above three steps with the next-to-last sentence. Continue this three-step analysis with each isolated sentence in reverse order until you end up at your first sentence last.

Stage Three: Correcting Your Sentences

In this chapter, there are two steps of this stage:

Step 1: Correct all incomplete sentences with a zero written in front of them. They are fragments, not complete thoughts. Each sentence must contain all five essential parts: a capital letter, a subject, a verb, a complete thought, and a period.

Step 2: Correct all crammed sentences with a two written in front of them. They are run-on sentences and must be clearly separated with a period, a semi-colon, or a comma before a FANBOYS word.

Stage Four: Returning Your Sentences to Paragraph Form for the Final Polish

To return your sentences to paragraph form, follow these two steps:

Step 1: Place your cursor in front of the last sentence and hit the backspace key as many times as needed until it is one space after the previous period. Repeat with each sentence. This action deletes the numbers. The following example illustrates how this looks in Microsoft Word.

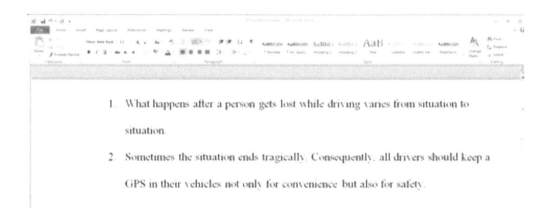

Step 2: Backspace your first sentence until it reaches the left margin. Press the tab key one time. Your sentences are now back together as a properly indented paragraph. Be sure to save your work.

If your instructor assigned a multi-paragraph essay, you will repeat all four stages of the proofreading process (isolating, analyzing, correcting, and returning) with every paragraph in your essay. Since you have already proofread your last paragraph, you are now ready to proofread your next-to-last paragraph. Continue proofreading in reverse order until you finish your first paragraph last. Be sure to save your work after proofreading each paragraph.

Polishing the Final Draft

After you have completed all four stages of the proofreading process for each paragraph, print out your final draft. Slowly read it aloud from beginning to end to make sure that you actually made all the changes you intended to make. You may find it even more helpful to get a friend to read it aloud slowly while you listen. Your friend will read it exactly the way it appears on the paper rather than the way you think you wrote it, thus making it easier for you to catch any further errors. This is your last chance to turn your paper into a polished final draft deserving of a high grade, so allow yourself enough time to proofread thoroughly.

CHAPTER 3

Separating Items in a List

In this chapter, you will learn how to proofread your papers to make each item in a list consistent with the other items in the list and to punctuate those items correctly. After you have successfully completed this chapter, you should be able to do the following:

- Analyze writings to determine if lists are consistent.
- Make each item in a list consistent with the other items.
- Recall and apply three rules to punctuate lists.
- Analyze writings to determine two major purposes for punctuation.
- Apply proofreading techniques to make sentences complete, separate, and consistent.

Identifying Items in a List

In Chapter 2, you recalled that the main purpose for punctuation is to separate two complete sentences. Another major purpose for punctuation is to separate items in a list. You were taught this second purpose when you were in elementary school but may not have been taught why you needed to separate the items. The reason is that punctuation marks let the reader know the exact number of items in a list. Without punctuation, the reader must guess the number and may not be correct. To illustrate, how many people are in the following list?

Unclear: Billy Jean Charlie and Tiffany are the new officers.

The reader may think there are four people:

1. Billy

2. Jean

3. Charlie

4. Tiffany

The writer, however, may have only three people in mind:

1. Billy Jean

2. Charlie

3. Tiffany

If the writer does have three people in mind, the sentence would be punctuated as follows:

Example: Billy Jean, Charlie, and Tiffany are the new officers of the Purposeful Punctuation Society.

If instead the writer has four people in mind, the sentence would be punctuated like this:

Example: Billy, Jean, Charlie, and Tiffany are the new officers of the Purposeful Punctuation Society.

Punctuation—as demonstrated in the examples above—tells readers how many items are in a list. Next, we will determine how to make those items flow smoothly in a sentence.

Matching Items in a List

When all items in a list are similar to each other, readers find that the list flows easily. To demonstrate, read through the four lists below.

1
Bill
Jean
Charlie
Tiffany

2
A subject
A verb
A complete thought

3
Planning
Drafting
Revising
Proofreading

4
Arguable thesis statement
Interesting content
Well-developed paragraphs
Clear organization
Perfect punctuation

Notice that in the first list all the items are people's names. In the second list, all the items begin with the letter *a* and end with a noun. In the third list, all the items end with *ing*. In the last list, all the items begin with a descriptive word and end with a noun. Because each item consistently matches the other items, it probably took you less than a minute to read all four lists.

The items in the lists of the following exercise, however, do not match each other and cause readers to stumble.

OBSERVATION 1

Directions:

1. Cross out the one item in each list that does not match the other items.

2. Re-word the crossed-out item so that it matches.

Example:

scrub both of the toilets

wash all of the dirty dishes

~~laundry~~   *clean all of the dirty clothes*

1. Robin
   Sparrow
   Bright red bird

© Tim Zurowski   © Hoang Mai Thach/Shutterstock.com   © David Byron Keener/Shutterstock.com

2. Food
   Drinking
   Smoking

3. Planning what to write
   Write the first draft
   Revise two or three drafts
   Proofread the final draft

4. To swim in the pool
   To hike through the woods
   Climb one mountain
   To run a marathon

5. Talk about anything and everything
   Travel to interesting places
   Who will read books instead of watching television

In academic writing, listings like the ones in the previous exercise are placed in a sentence rather than in a vertical list. Without the quick visual format of a list, it becomes even more important that each item in the list match up with the other items in the list (also known as a series). In the example below, each item in the list begins with the letter *a* and ends with a noun.

Example: Every sentence must contain **a subject**, **a verb**, and **a complete thought**.

In the next sentence, each item in the list (or series) begins with a descriptive word and ends with a noun.

Example: An excellent essay has an **arguable thesis statement**, **interesting content**, **well-developed paragraphs**, **clear organization**, and **perfect punctuation**.

OBSERVATION 2

Directions:

1. Cross out the one item in each list that does not match.

2. Re-write the crossed-out item so that it matches the other items.

Example:

I need to scrub both the toilets, wash all of the dirty dishes, and ~~laundry~~.
clean all of the dirty clothes

1. The most common birds in this area are robins, sparrows, and bright red ones.

2. She wants a companion who will talk about anything and everything, travel to interesting places, and who will read books instead of watching television all the time.

3. The four stages of the proofreading process are to isolate the sentences from the paragraph, analyzing each sentence individually, correcting sentences with errors, and returning the sentences to paragraph form.

4. No food, drinking, or smoking is allowed in the auditorium.

5. Writing requires one to plan, to draft, to revise, and proofreading.

Punctuating Items in a List

When you have a list of items, you need to make the items similar and separate them properly so that the sentence has a consistent flow for your readers. To separate items in a list, there are three punctuation rules to follow:

Rule #1: When the list is within the sentence, put commas between the items.

Rule #2: When the list is after the sentence, separate the sentence from the list with a colon.

Rule #3: When there is a list within a list, alternate the comma and the semi-colon.

PUNCTUATING A LIST WITHIN A SENTENCE

When a list is written as a vertical listing, the format identifies it as a list. When a list is written as part of a sentence, punctuation marks identify it as a list. Therefore, consistency in punctuating lists is just as important as consistency in matching the items.

Rule #1: When a list is **within** a sentence, put commas **between** the items.

Example: Billy, Jean, Charlie, and Tiffany are the new officers of the Purposeful Punctuation Society.

Example: The new officers of the Purposeful Punctuation Society are Billy, Jean, Charlie, and Tiffany.

Example: Planning, drafting, revising, and proofreading are the four stages of the writing process.

Example: The four stages of the writing process are planning, drafting, revising, and proofreading.

Note that no comma appears before the first item or after the last item. The commas in a listing appear only **between** the items.

This rule of separating items in a list with commas is also used for dates and addresses. In the next example, each item in the list is a separate item of a date: the day, the date itself, and the year.

Example: She was born on Tuesday, March 13, 1990.

In the final example of this rule, each item in the list is a separate item of an address: street, city, and state.

Example: The college is located at 700 North Drive, Henderson, Maryland.

OBSERVATION 1

Directions:

1. Circle each comma in the list.

2. In the blank line, write the total number of items the list contains.

Example:

_3_ This exercise contains commas, lists, and totals.

___ 1. The seasons of the year are spring, summer, fall, and winter.

___ 2. Cookies, pies, and ice cream taste better than cake.

___ 3. She prefers someone who is a great listener, a good cook, and a beautiful dancer.

___ 4. She wants a companion who will talk about anything and everything, who will travel to interesting places, and who will not watch television all the time.

___ 5. The four stages of the proofreading process are isolating the sentences from the paragraph, analyzing each sentence individually, correcting sentences with errors, and returning the sentences to paragraph form.

PREPARATION 1

Directions:

Put a comma between the items in each list.

Example:

This exercise contains items, lists, and commas.

1. A refrigerator a microwave and a toaster are permitted in some dorms.

2. Swimming biking and running are the three legs of a triathlon.

3. Participants swim a quarter of a mile bike ten miles and run three miles.

4. He plans to climb a mountain to hike through a forest and to visit three countries this year.

5. She is looking for someone who enjoys talking for hours shopping for name-brand clothes eating at expensive restaurants and paying for everything.

PREPARATION 2

Directions:

1. Put a comma between the items in each list.

2. Re-word the one item in each list that does not match the others.

Example:

Writing requires one to plan, to draft, to revise, and ~~proofreading~~.

to proofread

1. Food drinking and smoking are not allowed in the auditorium.

2. New Zealand rabbits can be solid white solid black or red.

3. Bright yellow dark yellow brown and light rust leaves fell from the tree.

4. She prefers running in the morning swim at lunch and relaxing in the evenings.

5. Marcus's friend advised him to get a haircut to wear a suit and act like a professional.

PREPARATION 3

Directions:

1. Read the last sentence first. If it does not contain a list, it is correct.

2. If it does contain a list, put a comma between each item in the list.

3. Proceed in reverse order through the rest of the paragraph.

First impressions count in a job interview. Wearing sloppy, revealing, ill-fitting, or mismatched clothes will detract from what the candidate has to say. Even if that person is well-qualified, he or she will not be hired. Besides dressing appropriately, the candidate should arrive on time, answer questions thoughtfully, and thank the interviewer. These actions make a good impression and often lead to getting the job.

OBSERVATION 2

Directions:

In the blank line, write the number of the purpose for the punctuation marks:

   #1 – to separate two complete sentences

   #2 – to separate items in a list

Example:

__#2__ This exercise asks you to read each sentence, determine the punctuation purpose, and write the purpose number in the blank.

__2__ 1. Writers plan, write, revise, and proofread their works.

__1__ 2. This book has covered the two major purposes for punctuation. There is one more purpose to cover.

__1__ 3. He wrote his paper in a short time, but he revised it for a long time.

__1__ 4. The job description calls for someone who can type quickly, organize efficiently, and communicate well.

__2__ 5. Selena has the right background for the job; moreover, she has a friendly demeanor.

PUNCTUATING A LIST AFTER A SENTENCE

Sometimes a list will appear after a sentence rather than within it. When that is the case, you still put commas between the items. In addition, follow the second rule.

Rule #2: When a list is **after** the sentence, separate the sentence from the list with a colon.

A colon looks like two stacked periods. The bottom period tells the reader that the sentence has ended; the top period tells the reader that a list is coming next. Notice that in each of the following examples a full sentence appears before the colon and the list.

Example: We elected the following new officers: Bill, Jean, Charlie, and Tiffany.

Example: Every sentence must contain these essential items: a capital letter, a subject, a verb, a complete thought, and a period.

Example: The writing process consists of four stages: planning, drafting, revising, and proofreading.

Example: An excellent essay has the following qualities: an arguable thesis statement, interesting content, well-developed paragraphs, clear organization, correct grammar, and perfect punctuation.

Example: This is Tim's birthday: Friday, October 13, 2001.

Example: Here is Tim's new address: 123 New Road, Lima, Ohio.

OBSERVATION 1

Directions:

1. Circle the colon in each sentence.

2. Underline the complete sentence that appears before the colon.

Example:

A short list of punctuation marks comes after this sentence: period, semicolon, comma, and question mark.

1. The Thanksgiving feast consisted of several favorite dishes: turkey, dressing, cranberry sauces, sweet potatoes, green bean casserole, pumpkin pie, and pecan pie.

2. The following people served as judges for the contest: Kathy Cornish, James Bird, Nanette Wren, and Hogan Hen.

3. Only three types of flowers bloomed in the garden: roses, lilies, and tulips.

4. The writing process consists of the following four stages: planning, writing, revising, and proofreading.

5. Every sentence contains these five elements: a capital letter, a subject, a verb, a complete thought, and a period.

PREPARATION 1

Directions:

1. Underline the complete sentence that appears before the list.

2. Separate the sentence from the list with a colon.

3. Put commas between the items in the list.

Example:

<u>This exercise contains the following</u>: colons, lists, and commas.

1. A triathlon consists of three legs swimming biking and running.

2. Participants must do the following activities swim a quarter of a mile bike ten miles and run three miles.

3. He plans to do the following activities this year climb a mountain hike through a forest and visit three countries.

4. Only these small appliances are allowed in the dorm a refrigerator a microwave and a toaster.

5. She is looking for someone who enjoys doing the following talking for hours shopping for name-brand clothes eating at expensive restaurants and paying for everything.

OBSERVATION 2

Directions:

Underline the sentence. If there is a colon, the sentence ends at the colon. If there is no colon, the sentence ends at the period.

Examples:

<u>A short list of punctuation marks comes after this sentence</u>: period, semicolon, comma, and question mark.

<u>The most frequently used punctuation marks are the period, semicolon, and comma.</u>

1. The Thanksgiving feast consisted of turkey, dressing, cranberry sauces, sweet potatoes, green bean casserole, pumpkin pie, and pecan pie.

2. The following people served as judges for the contest: Kathy Cornish, James Bird, Nanette Wren, and Hogan Hen.

3. Three types of flowers bloom in the garden: roses, lilies, and tulips.

4. The three types of flowers that bloom in the garden are roses, lilies, and tulips.

5. The winners are Marlene, Johnetta, and Kenny.

6. The following people are the winners: Marlene, Johnetta, and Kenny.

7. The winners are the following: Marlene, Johnetta, and Kenny.

8. Every sentence contains a capital letter, a subject, a verb, a complete thought, and a period.

9. The writing process consists of planning, writing, revising, and proofreading.

PREPARATION 2

1. Underline the words before the list.

2. If the underlined words are a complete sentence, add a colon.

3. If the underlined words are not a complete sentence, do not add a colon.

Examples:

<u>These are the names of her children</u>: Briana, Kiana, and Tiana.

<u>Her children's names are</u> Briana, Kiana, and Tiana.

1. She enjoys swimming, biking, and running.

2. She enjoys the following activities swimming, biking, and running.

3. She raises three colors of Dutch rabbits black, gray, and chocolate.

4. The Dutch rabbits she raises are black, gray, and chocolate.

5. He has to practice his speech, buy a new suit, and pack his suitcase.

PREPARATION 3

Directions:

1. Put commas between all of the items in each list.

2. If a complete sentence appears before the list, separate it from the list with a colon.

3. If the sentence is not complete until the list ends, do not insert a colon.

Examples:

These are the names of her children: Briana, Kiana, and Tiana.

Her children's names are Briana, Kiana, and Tiana.

1. He has to do the following before he leaves practice his speech buy a new suit and pack his suitcase.

2. Proofreading involves isolating each sentence in a paragraph analyzing each sentence correcting sentences with errors and returning the sentences to paragraph form.

3. Ben Cartwright had three sons Adam Hoss and Little Joe.

4. Ben Cartwright's sons were Adam Hoss and Little Joe.

5. Proofreading has four stages isolating each sentence in a paragraph analyzing each sentence correcting sentences with errors and returning the sentences to paragraph form.

PREPARATION 4

Directions:

1. Read the last sentence first. If it does not contain a list, it is correct.

2. If it does contain a list, put a comma between each item in the list.

3. If a complete sentence comes before the list, insert a colon.

4. Proceed in reverse order through the rest of the paragraph.

Several types of deciduous trees grow in the city park: maple oak poplar tulip and walnut. These trees attract visitors during all the seasons, but the fall season is the most popular. At that time, the leaves slowly change into a myriad of colors. Their beauty entices people to take long walks through the park gather the colorful leaves into large piles and jump into them.

OBSERVATION 3

In the blank line, write the number of the purpose for the punctuation marks:

> #1 – to separate two complete sentences

> #2 – to separate items in a list

_#1_ The first purpose for punctuation is to separate two sentences. The second purpose is to separate items in a series.

___ 1. The judges are seated on the stage. Their names are listed on the program.

___ 2. The judges are as follows: Merry, Terry, and Perry.

___ 3. Merry, Terry, and Perry are the judges.

___ 4. They have narrowed the winners to the final three photographs: the one on the top left, the one in the center, and the one in the bottom right.

___ 5. Merry and Terry think the photograph on the left should win first place, but Perry thinks the one in the center should win.

PUNCTUATING A LIST WITHIN A LIST

Occasionally, you may have a list within a list. In that case, follow rule #3:

Rule #3: When there is a list within a list, **alternate** the comma and the semicolon.

In the examples below, there is one list of people's names and a second list of the position each person holds.

Example: The new officers of the Purposeful Punctuation Society are Bill, president; Jean, vice-president; Charlie, secretary; and Tiffany, treasurer.

Example: The following people are the new officers of the Purposeful Punctuation Society: Bill, president; Jean, vice-president; Charlie, secretary; Tiffany, treasurer.

In the next examples, there is one list of course numbers and a second list of course titles.

Example: I am taking ENG 101, College Writing; MAT 150, College Algebra; PSY 100, Introduction to Psychology; HIS 108, United States History.

Example: I am taking the following courses: ENG 101, College Writing; MAT 150, College Algebra; PSY 100, Introduction to Psychology; HIS 108, United States History.

The next two examples both have a list of counties and a list of states.

Example: Abraham Lincoln lived in Hardin County, Kentucky; Perry County, Indiana; and Macon County, Illinois.

Example: Abraham Lincoln lived in three places during his childhood years: Hardin County, Kentucky; Perry County, Indiana; Macon County, Illinois.

The final examples contain a list of birthdates and a list of years.

Example: My children's birthdays are March 13, 1990; February 26, 1993; and April 5, 1995.

Example: My children were born on these dates: March 13, 1990; February 26, 1995; and April 5, 1995.

Notice that in the above examples, the first sentence in each pair does not have a colon because the sentence does not end until after the list. The second example in each pair does need a colon because it has a complete sentence before the list.

Mastering this third rule of separating lists within lists is not difficult, but it certainly looks like it is. Perhaps that is why many instructors are impressed whenever their students apply this rule correctly.

OBSERVATION 1

Directions:

1. Draw an oval around each comma and around the word group that tells which listing the commas are separating.

2. Draw a rectangle around each semicolon and around the word group that tells which listing the semicolons are separating.

Example:

The re-assigned positions are Savanna, goal-keeper; Keisha, striker; Hannah, sweeper.

1. The players' birthdays are May 11, 2000; August 30, 2001; April 20, 2002.

    Years   Dates

2. The players are Julius, pitcher; Julia, first base; Julian, second base; June, third base; and Julianna, catcher.

        Players' names   Baseball positions

3. In one week, he flew to Los Angles, California; Detroit, Michigan; Orlando, Florida; and Boston, Massachusetts.

        States   Cities

4. The winners are Kathy Cornish, third place; Dwight Hen, second place; and Juan Bird, first place.

        Winners' Names   Prize Positions

5. She has Dr. Rau, algebra; Professor Smith, English; Professor Garcia, history; and Dr. West, art.

        Courses   Instructors' Names

PREPARATION 1

Punctuate a list within another list by alternating between the comma and the semicolon.

The re-assigned positions are Savanna, goal-keeper; Keisha, striker; Hannah, sweeper.

1. Classes did not meet on October, 12 2015; November, 24 2015; and February 14 2016.

2. The starting players are Number 27, Mike Mann; Number 11, Larry Lane; Number 42, Josh Johnson; Number 5, Percy Pointer; and Number 38, Cain Crusher.

3. She has lived in London, Ohio; London, Texas; and London, England.

4. The four stages of the proofreading process are stage one, isolating the sentences from the paragraph; stage two, analyzing each sentence; stage three, correcting sentences with errors; stage four, returning the sentences to paragraph form.

5. Tickets cost $15, rear seats; $30, balcony seats; $45, front; and center seats.

OBSERVATION 2

1. Draw an arrow pointing to the colon that separates the sentence from the list.

2. Draw an oval around each comma and around the word group that tells what kind of items the commas are separating.

3. Draw a rectangle around each semicolon and around the word group that tells what kind of items the semicolons are separating.

Here are the re-assigned positions: Savanna, goal-keeper; Keisha, striker; Hannah, sweeper.

Soccer positions   Player's names

1. There are four stages of the proofreading process: stage one, isolating the sentences from the paragraph; stage two, analyzing each sentence; stage three, correcting sentences with errors; stage four, returning the sentences to paragraph form.

   Stage numbers   Stage processes

2. The following lists the players' birthdays: May 11, 2000; August 30, 2001; April 20, 2002.

   Years   Dates

3. These people will play the following positions: Julius, pitcher; Julia, first base; Julian, second base; June, third base; and Julianna, catcher.

   Players' names   Baseball positions

4. He flew to all of these places in one week: Los Angeles, California; Detroit, Michigan; Orlando, Florida; and Boston, Massachusetts.

   States   Cities

5. These are the winners of the pie-eating contest: Kathy Cornish, third place; Dwight Hen, second place; and Juan Bird, first place.

   Winners' Names   Prize Position

PREPARATION 2

Directions:

1. Separate the sentence from the lists with a colon.

2. Punctuate the list within the list by alternating between the comma and the semicolon.

Example:

Here are the re-assigned positions: Savanna, goal-keeper; Keisha, striker; Hannah, sweeper.

1. She has held four positions in this company one waste-water operator two water plant operator three engineering intern four chief engineer.

2. This is his schedule every Tuesday and Thursday 8:00 math 9:25 English 10:40 biology 1:00 music.

3. Classes will not meet on the following dates October 12 2018 November 24 2018 and February 14 2019.

4. The winners of the poetry contest are as follows in third place Mia Story in second place Preston Prose and in first place Natalie Poet.

5. He went to four different high schools in four years North High 2010-2011 South High 2011-2012 East High 2012-2013 West High 2013-2014.

PREPARATION 3

Directions:

1. If a sentence appears before the lists, insert a colon.

2. Punctuate the list within the list by alternating between the comma and the semicolon.

The re-assigned positions are Savanna, goal-keeper; Keisha, striker; Hannah, sweeper.

These are the re-assigned positions: Savanna, goal-keeper; Keisha, striker; Hannah, sweeper.

1. His rabbits are New Zealand solid black Dutch black and white and American solid white.

2. She raises three types of rabbits Dutch chocolate and white New Zealand solid white and American solid blue.

3. The four seasons in Florida are spring pleasant and hot summer humid and very hot fall humid and still hot winter cool to hot.

4. The dinner consists of an appetizer fried mushrooms a salad Caesar or spinach the main course steak and baked potato and a dessert chocolate lava cake with vanilla ice cream.

5. The dinner consists of four courses an appetizer fried mushrooms a salad Caesar or spinach the main course steak and baked potato and a dessert chocolate lava cake with vanilla ice cream.

PREPARATION 4

1. Read the last sentence first and work up to the first sentence last. If a sentence does not contain a list, it is correct.

2. If the sentence does contain a list within a list, punctuate it by alternating between the comma and the semicolon.

3. If there is a sentence before the lists, insert a colon.

Hosting a holiday meal involves a lot of preparation. Nanette planned ahead by asking families to bring the following dishes the Flores family drinks and breads the Eastridge family vegetables the Gray family desserts. Everyone agreed, so Nanette can now focus on all the other preparations. She must first bake the turkey and dressing second clean the house third set the table and decorate and fourth shower and dress for the occasion.

OBSERVATION 3

Directions:

In the blank line, write the number of the purpose for the punctuation marks:

> #1 – to separate two complete sentences

> #2 – to separate items in a list

Example:

_#2_ She is wearing three colors: black, gray, and lime green.

___ 1. Punctuation marks separate two complete sentences, and they separate items in a list.

___ 2. She enjoys reading, writing, and painting.

___ 3. Punctuation marks identify a list in a sentence; therefore, it is important to use them correctly.

___ 4. He has four children: the oldest, Julius; the second, Julia; the third, Julian; and the youngest, Julianna.

___ 5. His children's names are too similar. They all begin with the same four letters.

Proofreading to Separate Items in a List

APPLICATION 1

Directions:

1. Read the last sentence first. If it is does not contain a list, it is correct.

2. If the sentence does contain a list, insert commas between the items.

3. If the sentence contains a list with a list, alternate the comma and the semi-colon.

4. If there is a complete sentence before the list, insert a colon between the sentence and the list.

The ideal career has three important characteristics a flexible schedule a variety of duties and a friendly atmosphere. Some specific careers and fields that have these characteristics are pediatric nurse health elementary teacher education web-based owner business. The hours are good each day is different and the people are pleasant.

In the previous chapters, you learned how to find and correct fragments (incomplete sentences) and run-on sentences (two sentences crammed together). In this chapter, you have learned how to punctuate a sentence with a list. Now it is time to combine that knowledge and apply it to other writers' paragraphs and then to your own writing. To proofread others' writings, work through the following three stages:

1. Isolate the sentences from the paragraph.

2. Analyze each sentence to determine if it is an incomplete sentence, a sentence with a list, or two sentences run together.

3. Correct those sentences that are incomplete, inconsistent, and crammed together.

APPLICATION 2

Directions:

Stage 1:

Take a blank sheet of paper and cover up all the sentences in the paragraph below except the last one. Continue isolating the sentences in the paragraph by uncovering and reading from the last one up to the first one.

Stage 2:

As you read each isolated sentence aloud, ask yourself if it is an incomplete thought, an inconsistent list, or two sentences crammed together.

Stage 3:

If it is an incomplete thought, change it from a fragment into a complete sentence. You may wish to review Chapter 1. If it is two sentences crammed together, correct it by clearly separating the sentences with a period, a semicolon, or a comma before a coordinating conjunction. You may wish to review Chapter 2. If it is an inconsistent list, correct it by using the rules you learned in this chapter.

I may not look like a beaver, however, I certainly do act like one, Because I am always building remodeling or improving my home. So far I have built two homes, remodeled four others, and improved all of them. In my current home, I have already completed several remodeling projects in every room, stripped off layers of wallpaper, master bedroom, ripped out the 1980's hunter green carpeting, living room and bedrooms, repainted the cabinets kitchen and bathrooms, and refinished the hardwood floors living room and hallway. Some people may think I'm crazy, this inner drive to improve my home is just the beaver way of life.

APPLICATION 3

Stage 1:

Take a blank sheet of paper and cover up all the sentences in the paragraph below except the last one. Continue isolating the sentences in the paragraph by uncovering and reading from the last one up to the first one.

Stage 2:

As you read each isolated sentence aloud, ask yourself if it is an incomplete thought, an inconsistent list, or two sentences crammed together.

Stage 3:

If it is an incomplete thought, change it from a fragment into a complete sentence. You may wish to review Chapter 1. If it is two sentences crammed together, correct it by clearly separating the sentences with a period, a semicolon, or a comma before a coordinating conjunction. You may wish to review Chapter 2. If it is an inconsistent list, correct it by using the rules you learned in this chapter.

Re-designing a living room is a rewarding process. It can be accomplished in half a day with a few cleaning supplies broom vacuum cleaner window cleaning spray and dust cloths. The only items you may need to purchase are touch-up paint furniture moving pads and picture-hanging tools. The steps for redesigning the living room are one remove everything from the room two clean the windows and floor three apply touch-up paint on the walls four determine the room's focal point five arrange the seating around the focal point six position the rest of the furniture seven arrange items on the table surfaces eight hang pictures and artwork then you can relax and enjoy your newly re-designed living room.

APPLICATION 4

Finally, it is time for you to apply all of the information you have learned in this chapter and the previous ones to proofread your own paper. For your final draft, you will follow a four-stage proofreading process that will take about fifteen minutes per paragraph. The results will be well worth the time and effort.

Stage One: Isolating Your Sentences

To isolate the sentences in your own writing, follow these four steps:

Step 1: On a computer, open the final draft of your paper.

Step 2: Go to the beginning of the last paragraph and click on the numbering icon. The number 1 will appear in front of your paragraph. The following example illustrates where the icon and the number appear in Microsoft Word.

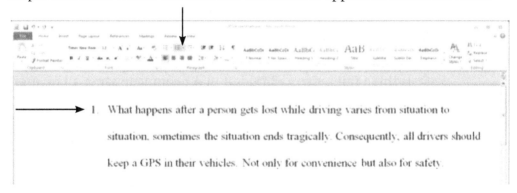

Step 3: Press the enter key after every period in the paragraph. This action will convert your paragraph into a list of individually numbered sentences. The following example illustrates how this looks in Microsoft Word.

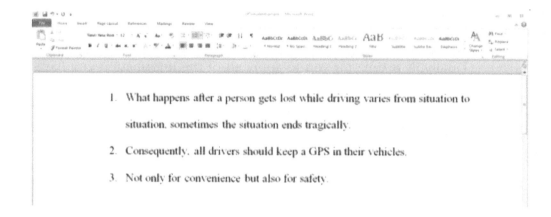

1. What happens after a person gets lost while driving varies from situation to situation. sometimes the situation ends tragically.

2. Consequently. all drivers should keep a GPS in their vehicles.

3. Not only for convenience but also for safety.

Step 4: Print out only the page that contains your isolated sentences.

Stage Two: Analyzing Your Sentences

To analyze each sentence of your paper, follow these four steps:

Step 1: Look at the last isolated sentence on your printed page. Slowly read it aloud, adding the words ***I realize*** to the beginning of the sentence. Ask yourself, "Is this a full sentence? Does it make complete sense all by itself?" Do **not** look at the sentence before it. If you cannot keep from peeking, then cover up the previous sentences with a sheet of paper. The sentence you are focusing on has to make sense without using the rest of the paragraph as a crutch. If it does not make sense by itself, write a zero in front of it.

> *0*   4. Not only for convenience but also for safety.

Step 2: If it is a complete sentence, ask yourself, "Does it contain a list?" If all the items in that list do not match each other or the listing is not punctuated correctly, write a one in front of it.

> *1*   2. A GPS is a navigation tool that directs travelers to any point of interest to a specific address and their own home.

Step 3: If the sentence is complete and consistent, then ask yourself, "Is it two complete thoughts crammed together?" If so, write a two in front of it.

2	1. What happens after a person gets lost while driving varies from situation to situation, sometimes the situation ends tragically.

Step 4: Repeat the above three steps with the next-to-last sentence. Continue this three-step analysis with each isolated sentence in reverse order until you end up at your first sentence last.

Stage Three: Correcting Your Sentences

To correct your errors, follow these three steps:

Step 1: Correct all incomplete sentences with a zero written in front of them. They are fragments, not complete thoughts. Each sentence must contain the five essentials: a capital letter, a subject, a verb, a complete thought, and a period.

Step 2: Correct all sentences with the number one written in front of them. They contain inconsistent lists. The items in these lists must match each other and be punctuated clearly.

Step 3: Correct all sentences with the number two written in front of them. They are run-on sentences and need to be clearly separated with a period, a semicolon, or a comma before a FANBOYS word.

Stage Four: Returning Your Sentences to Paragraph Form for the Final Polish

To return your sentences to paragraph form, follow these two steps:

Step 1: Place your cursor in front of the last sentence and hit the backspace key as many times as needed until it is one space after the previous period. Repeat with each sentence. This action deletes the numbers. The following example illustrates how this looks in Microsoft Word.

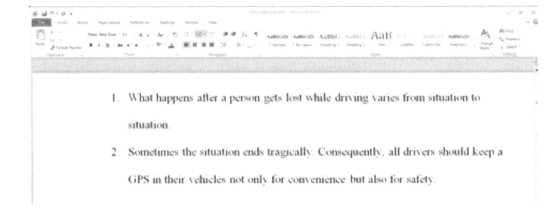

1. What happens after a person gets lost while driving varies from situation to situation.

2. Sometimes the situation ends tragically. Consequently, all drivers should keep a GPS in their vehicles not only for convenience but also for safety.

Step 2: Backspace your first sentence until it reaches the left margin. Press the tab key one time. Your sentences are now back together as a properly indented paragraph. Be sure to save your work.

If your instructor assigned a multi-paragraph essay, you will repeat all four stages of the proofreading process (isolating, analyzing, correcting, and returning) with every paragraph in your essay. Since you have already proofread your last paragraph, you are now ready to proofread your next-to-last paragraph. Continue proofreading in reverse order until you finish your first paragraph last. Be sure to save your work after proofreading each paragraph.

Polishing the Final Draft

After you have completed all four stages of the proofreading process for each paragraph, print out your final draft. Slowly read it aloud from beginning to end to make sure that you actually made all the changes you intended to make. You may find it even more helpful to get a friend to read it aloud slowly while you listen. Your friend will read it exactly the way it appears on the paper rather than the way you think you wrote it, thus making it easier for you to catch any further errors. This is your last chance to turn your paper into a polished final draft deserving of a high grade, so allow yourself enough time to proofread thoroughly.

CHAPTER 4

Separating Extra Information from the Main Thought

In this chapter, you will learn how to proofread your papers to make the main thought of each sentence clearly distinguishable from any extra information it may contain. After you have successfully completed this chapter, you should be able to do the following:

- Recognize the main thought of a sentence.
- Recognize extra information in a sentence.
- Determine the location of extra information in relation to the main thought.
- Recall and apply four rules of punctuation to clearly distinguish extra information from the main thought.
- Analyze writings to determine the three major purposes for punctuation.
- Apply proofreading techniques to make sentences complete, separate, consistent, and correct.

Identifying Extra Information

The main purpose for punctuation, as Chapter 2 reminds you, is to separate two complete thoughts. A second purpose for punctuation, as noted in Chapter 3, is to separate items in a list. The third major purpose for punctuation is to separate extra information from the sentence itself. This final purpose is an important one to recognize and apply because this separation allows readers to understand precisely how the writer intends for the sentence to be read.

Extra information simply means that the words are not part of the main thought. If you remove the extra information, the sentence would still be a complete thought that makes sense by itself.

Example: At last, James understands the main purposes for punctuation.

In the above example, the first two words are extra information. If removed, the sentence is still complete as shown in the example below:

Example: James understands the main purposes for punctuation.

To correctly punctuate sentences that contain extra information, you first need to determine where the extra information is in relation to the main thought. In the examples given below, the main sentence is in bold while the extra information remains in regular print. As you can see, extra information can be found at various positions.

At times, the extra information comes before the main thought.

Example: In the end, **she could not think of one good example**.

At other times, however, the extra information interrupts the sentence.

Example: **Savanna**, my youngest daughter, **is an artist**.

The extra information can be found after the main thought, too.

Example: **She went to the store with Bill**, her husband.

Punctuating Extra Information

Once you have determined the location of the extra information (before the sentence, interrupting the sentence, or after the sentence), then you can apply the appropriate rules. There are four:

Rule #1: When the extra information comes before the main thought, put a comma between the introductory words and the sentence.

Rule #2: When the extra information slightly interrupts the sentence, put a pair of commas around the interruption.

Rule #3: When the extra information strongly interrupts the sentence, put a pair of dashes or a pair of parentheses around the interruption.

Rule #4: When the extra information comes after the main thought, use a comma if the extra information needs no emphasis, a dash if it does need emphasis, or a colon if it is an explanation.

PUNCTUATING INTRODUCTORY INFORMATION

Writers often lead into a sentence with one or more introductory words. To make it clear to readers that those words are extra information, they need to be separated from the sentence itself. Without punctuation, the reader can become confused.

Unclear: When students proofread instructors find fewer errors.

At first, the reader may think that the students are proofreading their instructors. Since that does not make sense, the reader has to try to determine where the introductory material ends and the main thought begins.

Clear: When students proofread, instructors find fewer errors.

Readers do not like back-tracking or trying to figure out what the writer meant to say. As a writer yourself, you want your readers to know which part of what you have written is introductory information and which part is the actual sentence. To be clear, then, follow this rule:

Rule #1: When extra information comes **before** the main thought, put a comma between the introductory words and the main thought.

Sometimes introductory information is as short as a single word, as in the following examples:

Example: First, the reader must determine the location of the extra information.

Example: Fortunately, punctuation marks clear up confusing sentences.

OBSERVATION 1

Directions:

1. Draw a circle around the comma that separates the introductory information from the main thought.

2. Underline the main thought.

Example:

Generally (,) that restaurant serves hundreds of customers a day.

1. First, a writer must have a purpose for writing.

2. Next, the writer needs to come up with an organizational plan.

3. Additionally, he will need to write convincing details.

4. Finally, she has finished writing her essay.

5. Nevertheless, the writer still needs to proofread his final draft.

PREPARATION 1

1. Underline the main thought.

2. Put a comma between the introductory word and the main thought.

Example:

Finally, <u>the rules for punctuation are clear</u>.

1. Obviously the sun rises in the east and sets in the west.

2. Naturally parents want their children to be happy.

3. First the members elected officers for their new club.

4. Next they held their first meeting.

5. Lately Rick has been working on a new painting.

Introductory information may also be a few words long. Together, these words are called a phrase. Two types of introductory phrases that you need to recognize are signal phrases and prepositional phrases.

Signal phrases tell the reader who stated the complete thought that accompanies it. As with all introductory phrases, a signal phrase is separated from the sentence with a comma.

Example: The author claims, "Punctuating sentences is easy."

Prepositional phrases start with a pre**position** (a word that indicates position) and end with a noun or pronoun. To help you remember prepositional phrases, think of a mouse's position in relation to a group of houses.

A mouse can be in any number of positions:

in a house	under the ground
around a house	to the house
between two houses	through a window
among three houses	out the door
on the roof	from the house

Whenever you see a prepositional phrase before a main thought, separate it from the sentence with a comma, as in the following examples:

Example: In this example, the extra information comes before the sentence.

Example: Of course, the word **of** is one preposition that does not indicate position like the other prepositions do.

OBSERVATION 2

Directions:

1. Draw a circle around the comma that separates the introductory information from the main thought.

2. Underline the main thought.

Examples:

On Saturdays , the restaurant serves hundreds of customers.

Dr. Ima Quack states , "Rainy weather makes people happy."

1. At the crime scene, the police surrounded the area with yellow tape.

2. In front of the house, the neighbors waited to hear the full story.

3. The police claimed, "We have apprehended the criminals."

4. Of all the witnesses, only one had been close enough to hear the criminals' conversation.

5. From miles around, people descended upon the small town.

PREPARATION 2

Directions:

1. Underline the main thought.

2. Put a comma between the introductory phrase and the sentence.

Example:

In the future, <u>punctuating sentences will be easier</u>.

1. At this time the members will vote for their president.

2. In a few minutes they will announce their decision.

3. Upon further reflection she decided to keep her slightly damaged purchase.

4. The president proclaims "Change is good."

5. Of course the residents had to evacuate the burning building.

Introductory information can also be several words long. It may even contain a subject and a verb, but the thought will be incomplete. As pointed out in Chapter 1, incomplete thoughts often begin with SUBWAI words (subordinating conjunctions).

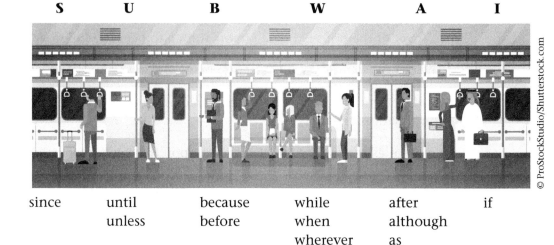

S	**U**	**B**	**W**	**A**	**I**
since	until	because	while	after	if
	unless	before	when	although	
			wherever	as	

© ProStockStudio/Shutterstock.com

When an incomplete thought comes before the main thought, separate it from the sentence with a comma. That comma lets the reader know that introductory information is in front of the main thought.

Example: After the extra information is given, the main thought is stated.

Example: If a sentence is unclear, many readers will stop reading.

OBSERVATION 3

Directions:

1. Draw an oval around the SUBWAI word (subordinating conjunction) that begins the extra information.

2. Draw a circle around the comma that separates the introductory information from the main thought.

3. Underline the main thought.

Example:

(When) introductory information comes first(,) separate it from the main thought with a comma.

1. After a long day at work, many people like to relax in their recliners.

2. When dog owners return home, their dogs greet them with exuberance.

3. Because he procrastinated, Tyrone made a failing grade on his writing assignment.

4. Although he submitted a paper, it did not meet the standards of effective communication.

5. If extra information comes before a sentence, a writer must put a comma between that introductory information and the main thought.

PREPARATION 3

Directions:

1. Draw an oval around the SUBWAI word (subordinating conjunction) that begins the extra information.

2. Underline the main thought.

3. Put a comma between the introductory information and the main thought.

Example:

(Although) punctuation rules seem complicated, they become simple after learning the three main purposes for punctuation.

1. Because each painting takes a full month to complete the cost is rather high.

2. Until one understands the reasons for punctuation the rules of punctuation will not make sense.

3. Since it is getting late we will finish this lesson tomorrow.

4. Whenever it is raining she feels sad and lonely.

5. As long as the sun is shining they will continue working outside.

We have now seen that introductory information can be a single word, a phrase, or an incomplete thought. Regardless of the length of the extra information, the same rule still applies: separate the extra, introductory information from the main thought with a comma.

OBSERVATION 4

Directions:

1. Draw a circle around the comma that separates the introductory information from the main thought.

2. Underline the main sentence.

Example:

Although it takes time, proofreading is worth the effort.

1. Furthermore, the writer gains a greater sense of accomplishment.

2. At last, she understood how to proofread her own work.

3. From the beginning, their relationship was based on friendship.

4. Jeremiah confessed, "I've always loved you."

5. When you write introductory information, you must separate the introduction from the main thought with a comma.

PREPARATION 4

Directions:

1. Read the last sentence first. If it does not contain introductory information, it is correct.

2. If the sentence does contain introductory information, put a comma between the extra information and the main thought; then underline the sentence.

3. Proceed in reverse order through the rest of the paragraph.

Writing an essay is like creating a work of art. First the writer must decide what to write. After sketching out a plan the writer, then follows that plan. Once the rough draft is finished it is best to set the work aside for a couple of days. When the writer returns, he or she begins revising the essay to improve the content. Finally the writer carefully proofreads it to eliminate any errors.

OBSERVATION 5

Directions: In the blank line, write the number of the purpose for the punctuation marks:

   #1 – to separate two complete sentences

   #2 – to separate items in a list

   #3 – to separate extra information from the sentence

Example:

 _#3_ In this exercise, you will identify the punctuation purpose of each sentence.

___ 1. This exercise asks you to identify the first punctuation purpose, separating two complete sentences; the second punctuation purpose, separating items in a series; and the third punctuation purpose, separating extra information from the sentence.

___ 2. After a long day of working in the hot sun, nothing feels better than a shower.

___ 3. The days were warmer than normal this winter; unfortunately, they were also hotter than normal this summer.

___ 4. In the summer, the temperatures sometimes soar above 100 degrees.

___ 5. Some days are too hot, and other days are too cold.

PUNCTUATING SLIGHT INTERRUPTIONS

Writers often begin a sentence with a subject and follow it immediately with the verb. Sometimes, though, a writer will add some extra information between the subject and verb. Typically, that extra information will be one of the following:

- A description of the subject
- Another name for the subject
- A transitional expression
- A signal phrase

To make it clear to the reader that extra information is interrupting the sentence, follow this rule:

Rule #2: When the extra information **slightly interrupts** the sentence, put a pair of commas around the interruption.

Examples of interruptions that describe the subject:

Zambia and Zimbabwe, which are in Africa, share Victoria Falls.

The reader, confused and frustrated, gave up.

Examples of interruptions that re-name the subject:

Briana, my oldest daughter, is a writer.

The sixteenth president, Abraham Lincoln, was assassinated in 1865.

Examples of interruptions that are transitional expressions:

The reader, however, was confused by the writer's statement.

The writer, therefore, decided to clear up the confusion.

Example of an interruption that signals who made the statement:

"Punctuating sentences," claims the author, "is easy."

If we take out the slight interruptions in the above examples, the sentences still make complete sense:

Example: Zambia and Zimbabwe share Victoria Falls.

Example: The reader gave up.

Example: Briana is a writer.

Example: The sixteenth president was assassinated in 1865.

Example: The reader was confused by the writer's statement.

Example: The writer decided to clear up the confusion.

Example: "Punctuating sentences is easy."

OBSERVATION 1

Directions:

1. Cross out the extra information that interrupts the sentence.

2. Underline the main sentence.

A good writer, ~~therefore~~, needs to be a good proofreader.

1. Floods and damaging storms, which are natural disasters, cannot be prevented.

2. Fires, however, can be prevented.

3. The ice storm, unfortunately, destroyed most of the trees in the county.

4. An unprecedented number of homeowners, of course, filed claims last year.

5. "We will definitely," assured the insurance agent, "take care of all claims in the most efficient manner possible."

PREPARATION 1

Directions:

1. Underline the main sentence.

2. Put a pair of commas around the slight interruption.

Example:

These sentences, you see, need commas around the interruption.

1. All modes of transportation of course have pros and cons.

2. Subway trains which move quickly provide efficient transportation at relatively low prices.

3. Mass transit moreover is reliable.

4. Private vehicles on the other hand are the only means of transportation in small cities and towns.

5. "All commuters" said the mayor "need more travel options."

PREPARATION 2

Some of the sentences below have extra information before the main thought begins, and some have extra information that interrupts the sentence.

1. First, underline the main sentence.

2. If the extra information is before the sentence, separate it with one comma.

3. If the extra information interrupts the sentence, separate it with a pair of commas.

Examples:

In the future, <u>punctuating sentences will be easier</u>.

<u>A good writer</u>, of course, <u>is also a good</u> proofreader.

1. The youngest child as everyone can tell picked out his own clothes.

2. Naturally his mother tried to get him to change his clothes.

3. The little boy nevertheless refused to change his shirt.

4. The clothes in his opinion look great together.

5. Although it rained briefly most of the day was sunny and pleasant.

PREPARATION 3

Directions:

1. Read the last sentence first. If it does not contain an interruption, it is correct.

2. If the sentence does contain an interruption, put a pair of commas around the interruption.

3. Proceed in reverse order through the rest of the paragraph.

The summer months provide opportunities for families to do more activities together. Vacationing on or near water of course is common. Those families however that cannot leave town enjoy swimming at a local pool. The high temperatures though drive a lot of people indoors. Many places as a result offer free movies during the summer.

PREPARATION 4

Directions:

1. Read the last sentence first. If it does not contain extra information, it is correct.

2. If the extra information is before the sentence, separate it with one comma.

3. If the extra information interrupts the sentence, put a pair of commas around the interruption.

4. Proceed in reverse order through the rest of the paragraph.

When new students attend freshmen orientation they are better prepared to face the challenges of their first semester. They already know for example what resources are available on campus. In addition they know where those resources are located. The students who do not attend orientation on the other hand often feel lost and confused.

OBSERVATION 2

In the blank line, write the number of the purpose for the punctuation marks:

    #1 – to separate two complete sentences

    #2 – to separate items in a list

    #3 – to separate extra information from the sentence

Example:

_#3_ This exercise, of course, asks you to identify the punctuation purpose of each sentence.

___ 1. The family built a sand castle, splashed in the water, and ate a picnic lunch.

___ 2. Sea gulls started snatching their food, so the family ran to an indoor shelter.

___ 3. Without sea gulls to annoy them, the family enjoyed their lunch.

___ 4. The sea gulls, however, wished the family had stayed outside.

___ 5. The family returned to the beach the next day; however, they brought a screened canopy with them.

PUNCTUATING STRONG INTERRUPTIONS

Have you ever been in a conversation with someone when you abruptly interrupted yourself to say something else before finishing your sentence? If so, you knew that you were throwing in a strong interruption. Your listener also knew which part was the interruption and which part was the real sentence. How? You changed the tone of your voice during the interruption. If the interruption was a command to someone else, your voice may have become louder: "Alisha, stop that!" If the interruption was a memory, your voice may have become softer: "That was before we lost everything in the tornado." Perhaps you simply stated your interruption in a different tone of voice.

Writers, obviously, cannot speak to their readers. Therefore, they must use punctuation marks to "speak" for them so their readers will recognize strong interruptions.

Rule #3: When the extra information **strongly interrupts** the sentence, put a pair of dashes or a pair of parentheses around the interruption.

Example: Abraham Lincoln (1809-1865) was the sixteenth president of the United States.

Example: Abraham Lincoln—who lived from 1809 to 1865—was the sixteenth president of the United States.

Example: The writer learned (much to his teacher's delight) how to use punctuation marks.

Example: The writer learned—much to his teacher's delight—how to use punctuation marks.

Example: A registered nurse (RN) has numerous responsibilities.

As with slight interruptions, when a strong interruption (the extra information inside the pair of parentheses or dashes) is removed, the sentence still makes sense.

Example: Abraham Lincoln was the sixteenth president of the United States.

Example: The writer learned how to use punctuation marks.

Example: A registered nurse has numerous responsibilities.

Although a pair of dashes and a pair of parentheses both signal to the reader that a strong interruption is enclosed within them, they each have distinct tones of voice. Use the pair of parentheses to indicate that the interruption is to be read in a softer voice than the sentence itself. Use the pair of dashes to indicate that the interruption is to be read in a louder or different voice than the sentence itself.

Dashes = **d**ifferent voice

Parenthe**ses** = **s**ofter voice

OBSERVATION 1

Directions:

1. Cross out the extra information that interrupts the sentence.

2. Underline the sentence.

Examples:

<u>A good writer</u> (~~as one might well expect~~) <u>is also a good proofreader.</u>

<u>A good writer</u> ~~as one might well expect~~—<u>is also a good proofreader.</u>

1. The doctor (the one who specializes in internal organs) recommends surgery.

2. A devastating tornado—F4 on the scale—touched down in several counties.

3. The governor (who had been in office only one day) declared a state of emergency.

4. The doctor—the one who specializes in internal organs—recommends surgery.

5. A devastating tornado (F4 on the scale) touched down in several counties.

PREPARATION 1

Directions:

1. Underline the sentence.

2. Put a pair of dashes around the interruption.

A good writer—as one might expect—is also a good proofreader.

1. Punctuating sentences believe it or not is not too difficult.

2. The Dutch rabbit though identical in markings is larger than the American Dutch.

3. He became a licensed practical nurse LPN last year.

4. Those three women Samantha, Savannah, and Emma have been friends since childhood.

5. Bright pink phlox a flowering ground cover spread down the hill.

PREPARATION 2

Directions:

1. Underline the sentence.

2. Put a pair of parentheses around the interruption.

Example:

A good writer (as one might expect) is also a good proofreader.

1. Punctuating sentences believe it or not is not too difficult.

2. The Dutch rabbit though identical in markings is larger than the American Dutch.

3. He became a licensed practical nurse LPN last year.

4. Those three women Samantha, Savannah, and Emma have been friends since childhood.

5. Bright pink phlox a flowering ground cover spread down the hill.

PREPARATION 3

Directions:

1. Underline the sentence.

2. Add a pair of parentheses around the interruption if you want the reader to use a softer tone. Add a pair of dashes around the interruption if you want the reader to use a different tone.

Examples:

A good writer—as one might expect—is also a good proofreader.

A good writer (as one might expect) is also a good proofreader.

1. Several cases particularly those without DNA evidence remain unsolved.

2. The most important issue contrary to popular opinion is not the economy.

3. The grade should but does not always reflect the quality of the paper.

4. All of the houses on one block the block surrounded by chain-link fencing have been condemned.

5. Dozens of hungry goldfinch which are green in the winter flocked to the bird feeder in the back yard

PREPARATION 4

Directions:

Some of the sentences below have extra information that slightly interrupts the sentence. Others have extra information that strongly interrupts the sentence.

1. Underline the sentence.

2. If the extra information is a slight interruption, put a pair of commas around it.

3. If the extra information is a strong interruption, put a pair of dashes or a pair of parentheses around it.

<u>A good writer</u>, of course, <u>must become a good proofreader.</u>

<u>A good writer</u> (as one might expect) <u>must become a good proofreader.</u>

1. Chloe the Yorkie yaps at everybody and everything.

2. The dog's owner unfortunately does not know how to train her.

3. The dog ran after a stranger someone who was out jogging and bit him.

4. Zoe the Doberman Pinscher rarely ever barks.

5. She is to everyone's surprise a sweet and gentle dog.

PREPARATION 5

Directions:

1. Read the last sentence first. If it does not contain an interruption, it is correct.

2. If the extra information is a slight interruption, put a pair of commas around it.

3. If the extra information is a strong interruption, put a pair of dashes or a pair of parentheses around it.

4. Proceed in reverse order through the rest of the paragraph.

Making scale models whether of buildings or of vehicles is a time-consuming but fun hobby. The most time-consuming models of course are the ones built entirely from scratch.

The builder spends several hours researching and designing the model before beginning construction. Gathering natural materials and purchasing others in general takes a few hours to a few days. The actual construction the fun part can vary from weeks to months.

PREPARATION 6

Directions:

1. Read the last sentence first. If it does not contain extra information, it is correct.

2. If extra information is before the sentence, separate it with one comma.

3. If extra information slightly interrupts the sentence, put a pair of commas around the interruption.

4. If extra information strongly interrupts the sentence, put a pair of dashes or a pair of parentheses around it.

5. Proceed in reverse order through the rest of the paragraph.

Making scale models whether of buildings or of vehicles is a time-consuming but fun hobby. Of course the most time-consuming models are the ones built entirely from scratch. Even before construction the builder must spend several hours researching and designing the model. Gathering natural materials and purchasing others in general takes a few hours to a few days. The actual construction the fun part can vary from weeks to months. Ultimately the hobbyist will have a model that looks almost identical to its full-size equivalent.

OBSERVATION 2

Directions:

In the blank line, write the number of the purpose for the punctuation marks:

#1 – to separate two complete sentences

#2 – to separate items in a list

#3 – to separate extra information from the sentence

Example:

__#3__ This exercise—it comes as no surprise—asks you to identify the punctuation purpose.

___ 1. She had a swollen abdomen, could not eat or drink, and was in continual pain.

___ 2. Although the patient had all of the symptoms of appendicitis, the doctor thought she was too old to have that illness.

___ 3. Another doctor—one with much more experience—recognized the problem.

___ 4. The patient had appendicitis, so the doctor recommended surgery.

___ 5. The surgery, unfortunately, revealed more issues.

PUNCTUATING ENDING INFORMATION

A popular joke reads as follows:

Let's eat Grandma.
Let's eat, Grandma.
Punctuation saves lives.

While punctuation may not actually be capable of saving lives, it does tell readers how to interpret a sentence. The first sentence in the above joke means that we are cannibals. The second sentence means that we are inviting Grandma to eat with us; the word "Grandma" is simply extra information after the main thought: "Let's eat."

We have seen that extra information can be placed before or in the middle of a sentence. Now we see that extra information can also be placed at the end of a sentence. Sometimes that extra information will need to be emphasized, but often it will not. At other times, that extra information will serve to explain the main thought. To make it clear to the reader which type of extra information is coming, follow this rule:

Rule #4: When the extra information comes after the main thought, use a comma if the extra information needs no emphasis, a dash if it needs emphasis, or a colon if it is an explanation.

In the two examples below, the extra information after the main thought does not need to be emphasized.

Example: Punctuate this sentence correctly, Tiffany.

Example: "Punctuating sentences is easy," claims the author.

OBSERVATION 1

Directions:

1. Circle the comma that separates the sentence from the extra information.

2. Underline the main thought.

Example:

<u>She is his wife</u>, Elise.

1. Zeke has two sons, James and John.

2. They own and manage the Double J, a cattle ranch.

3. They live outside of Boulder, Colorado.

4. Elise's birthday is November 4, 1977.

5. She works at First National, the new bank.

PREPARATION 1

Directions:

1. Underline the main thought.

2. Put a comma between the sentence and the extra information.

Example:

<u>They live in Middleboro</u>, which is between Bigville and Littleton.

1. You need to proofread your essay systematically Juanita.

2. They ate at the Clam Shack a popular restaurant.

3. Revising and proofreading are two different activities of course.

4. He has an appointment with Dr. Carlisle his English professor.

5. They are competing with the local team which has the hometown advantage.

Sometimes the extra information after a sentence is strongly emphasized. In those cases, a dash is placed between the main thought and the extra information. That dash tells the reader to read the extra information in a different and more emphatic voice, as in the following two examples.

Example: There is only one excuse for missing class—death.

Example: The reader came up with a plan for reading the poorly written essay—give up.

OBSERVATION 2

Directions:

1. Circle the dash that separates the sentence from the extra information.

2. Underline the main thought.

Example:

The little boy stuffed his sister's candy in his mouth—all four pieces.

1. The couple announced their engagement—at long last.

2. They are happy—very happy.

3. They have a great plan for their honeymoon—a secret destination.

4. They are going on a honeymoon to a secret location—remote and unknown to most people.

5. We felt like turkeys ourselves after our Thanksgiving feast—stuffed turkeys.

PREPARATION 2

Directions:

1. Underline the main thought.

2. Put a comma between the sentence and the extra information if no emphasis is needed.

3. Put a dash between the sentence and the extra information if it does need to be emphasized.

The car suddenly started rolling down the hill—without a driver.

1. The carnival ride spun faster alarmingly faster.

2. Please send this document by air mail sir.

3. They gingerly tiptoed down the stairs lips tightly shut.

4. They heard an unusual noise which startled them.

5. They turned around and ran back up the stairs eyes as big as saucers.

Finally, extra information after the main thought may provide an explanation. Typically, a word indicating a number will be in the main thought. When you have a sentence with a number word in it and explanatory information afterwards, put a colon after the sentence. Think of the colon as a "stacked period." The period on the bottom tells the reader that the sentence has ended. The period on the top announces that an explanation is next.

Example: The instructor told the students **a** secret: punctuation is simple.

Example: One should proofread **both** types of writings: paragraphs and essays.

OBSERVATION 3

Directions:

1. Circle the colon that separates the main thought from the extra information.

2. Underline the sentence.

3. Circle the number word in the sentence.

Example:

She wanted (two) things in life (:) fame and fortune.

1. He has one wish: to make an A on his paper.

2. She wrote two papers: narrative and descriptive.

3. These rules illustrate one purpose for punctuation: separate extra information from the main sentence.

4. Mark Twain made the following observation: "Kindness is the language which the deaf can hear and the blind can see."

5. Punctuation has a purpose: making the meaning clear to the readers.

PREPARATION 3

Directions:

1 Underline the main thought.

2. Put a comma between the sentence and the extra information if no emphasis is needed.

3. Put a dash between the sentence and the extra information if it does need to be emphasized.

4. Put a colon between the sentence and the extra information if it is an explanation.

Example:

<u>There are two parts to learning about punctuation</u>: its purposes and its rules.

1. He lives is Littleton which is a little town.

2. Two character traits are evident in Steve honesty and kindness.

3. He eats scrambled eggs for breakfast half a dozen daily.

4. They are taking the same course Fundamentals of Writing.

5. She sent an e-mail to Jamie her best friend.

OBSERVATION 4

In the blank line, write the number of the purpose for the punctuation marks:

#1 – to separate two complete sentences

#2 – to separate items in a list

#3 – to separate extra information from the sentence

<u>#3</u> This exercise asks you to identify the punctuation purpose, of course.

___ 1. She has revised her paper; however, she still needs to proofread it.

___ 2. There is an underlying reason for punctuation: clarity.

___ 3. She plans to finish college, work in a law firm, and run for political office.

___ 4. They are eating at the new Mexican restaurant, Acapulco.

___ 5. Their strengths—great food and great service—make them popular.

Proofreading to Separate Extra Information from the Main Thought

APPLICATION 1

1. Read the last sentence first. If it does not contain extra information, it is correct.

2. If the extra information does not need to be emphasized, separate it with a comma.

3. If the extra information does need to be emphasized, separate it with a dash.

4. If the extra information explains the sentence, separate it with a colon.

5. Proceed in reverse order through the rest of the paragraph.

Lisa likes all kinds of desserts especially chocolate desserts. Her two favorite desserts are both chocolate lava cake and brownies. A plain brownie is not good enough though. It has to have chocolate frosting on top lots and lots of frosting.

APPLICATION 2

Directions:

1. Read the last sentence first. If it does not contain extra information, it is correct.

2. If extra information is before the sentence, separate it with one comma.

3. If extra information is after the sentence, separate it with a comma if it needs no emphasis, a dash if it does need emphasis, and a colon if it is an explanation.

4. Proceed in reverse order through the rest of the paragraph.

Three young women sit at a table in a restaurant. Although they are together they are not connected to each other. Instead they are on their cell phones. They do not talk into their phones though. They do only two things text messaging and web surfing. Socializing with the people around them appears to be an art a lost art.

APPLICATION 3

Directions:

1. Read the last sentence first. If it does not contain extra information, it is correct.

2. If extra information is before the sentence, separate it with one comma.

3. If extra information slightly interrupts the sentence, put a pair of commas around the interruption.

4. If extra information strongly interrupts the sentence, put a pair of dashes or a pair of parentheses around it.

5. If extra information is after the sentence, separate it with a comma if it needs no emphasis, a dash if it does need emphasis, and a colon if it is an explanation.

6. Proceed in reverse order through the rest of the paragraph.

You will now illustrate one of the primary purposes for punctuation to separate extra information from the main sentence. In this sentence the extra information is at the beginning. This next sentence however has the extra information interrupting the sentence. This sentence perhaps the hardest one to punctuate has a strong interruption.

You can now call yourself a genius a punctuation genius.

In the previous chapters, you learned how to find and correct fragments (incomplete sentences), run-on sentences (two sentences crammed together), and inconsistent lists. In this chapter, you have learned how to make the meaning of a sentence clear to the readers by separating extra information from the main thought. Now it is time to combine all of that knowledge and apply it to other writers' paragraphs and then to your own writing. While that sounds like a large number of errors to watch for while proofreading, it is manageable if you do it in the following three stages:

Stage 1: Isolate the sentences from the paragraph.

Stage 2: Analyze each sentence to determine if it is an incomplete sentence, one inconsistent or unclear sentence, or two sentences crammed together.

Stage 3: Correct only those sentences that are incomplete, inconsistent, unclear, and crammed together.

APPLICATION 4

Directions:

Stage 1:

Take a blank sheet of paper and cover up all the sentences in the paragraph below except the last one. Continue isolating all the sentences in the paragraph by uncovering and reading from the last one up to the first one.

Stage 2:

As you read each isolated sentence aloud, ask if it is an incomplete thought, an inconsistent or unclear sentence, or two sentences crammed together.

Stage 3:

If it is an incomplete thought, change it from a fragment into a sentence. You may wish to review Chapter 1. If it is a sentence with an inconsistent list, make the items in the list consistent and then punctuate. You may wish to review Chapter 3. If it is an unclear sentence, make it clear by separating the extra information from the main thought, as explained in this chapter. If it is two sentences crammed together, correct it by clearly separating the sentences. You may wish to refer to Chapter 2.

Fortunately careers in social work and in elementary education both provide opportunities for advancement. A social worker can start as a case worker and move up to the position of director the highest position. The advancement path in elementary education is the following teacher's aide teacher assistant principal head principal. Top positions however require advanced degrees.

APPLICATION 5

Directions:

Stage 1:

Take a blank sheet of paper and cover up all the sentences in the paragraph below except the last one. Continue isolating all the sentences in the paragraph by uncovering and reading from the last one up to the first one.

Stage 2:

As you read each isolated sentence aloud, ask if it is an incomplete thought, an inconsistent or unclear sentence, or two sentences crammed together.

Stage 3:

If it is an incomplete thought, change it from a fragment into a sentence. You may wish to review Chapter 1. If it is a sentence with an inconsistent list, make the items in the list consistent and then punctuate. You may wish to review Chapter 3. If it is an unclear sentence, make it clear by separating the extra information from the main thought, as explained in this chapter. If it is two sentences crammed together, correct it by clearly separating the sentences. You may wish to refer to Chapter 2.

Single parents should choose a career that fits their lifestyle has a pleasant work environment and pays well. The first factor to consider is lifestyle. Because single parents need to be home when their children get home from school. Their career should have either fixed daytime hours or flexible work-at-home hours. Secondly a pleasant work environment is important to a person's mental health. A single parent has enough stress at home, she doesn't need more stress at work. The most important characteristic of an ideal career for a single parent though is the pay. Without the income of a spouse a single parent needs to make enough money to take care of all expenses.

APPLICATION 6

Finally, it is time for you to apply all of the information you have learned in this chapter and the previous ones to proofread your own paper. Proceed to the next chapter (which happens to be the last one) to learn how to implement all four stages of proofreading to your final draft.

CHAPTER 5

Proofreading Your Final Draft

After you have successfully completed this chapter, you should be able to do the following:

- Apply the four stages of proofreading to your own writings.
- Apply the three major purposes for punctuation to your own writings.

Four Stages of Proofreading

Novice and professional writers alike find the task of proofreading their final drafts challenging. Because the mind knows what the writer intended to write, the eye can no longer see existing mistakes when it is time to proofread. The key, then, to proofreading is to approach the paper in an entirely different order. Instead of reading from beginning to end as a unified piece of writing, you will find it helpful to read your paper from the end to the beginning as individually isolated sentences. When focusing on each sentence in isolation, you can then determine if it is complete and clear. Additionally, you can determine why and what punctuation is needed. After correcting all errors, you will return the sentences to paragraph form to read one final time before submitting your work. To summarize, then, the four stages of this proofreading system are as follows:

Stage 1: Isolate your sentences one paragraph at a time.

Stage 2: Analyze your sentences in reverse order.

Stage 3: Correct each sentence that is incomplete, inconsistent, unclear, or crammed into another sentence.

Stage 4: Return your sentences to paragraph form for the final polish.

Obviously, this four-stage proofreading system does take time, so be sure that you budget an adequate amount to complete the full process. In the end, you will find that the results—clearly written papers, higher grades, and greater self-confidence in your writing ability—are well worth the extra effort.

STAGE ONE: ISOLATING SENTENCES FROM THE PARAGRAPH

The first stage of the proofreading system is to isolate your sentences one paragraph at a time. Allow approximately two minutes per paragraph to complete this stage.

Step 1: Move your cursor to the beginning of the last paragraph of your paper and click.

Step 2: Click on the numbering icon displayed in the paragraph section of the menu bar. The number 1 will appear in front of your last paragraph. The following example illustrates how this looks in Microsoft Word.

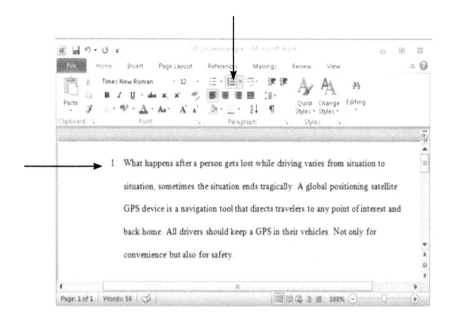

Step 3: Press the enter key after every period in the paragraph. This action will convert your paragraph into a list of individually numbered sentences. The following example illustrates how this looks in Microsoft Word.

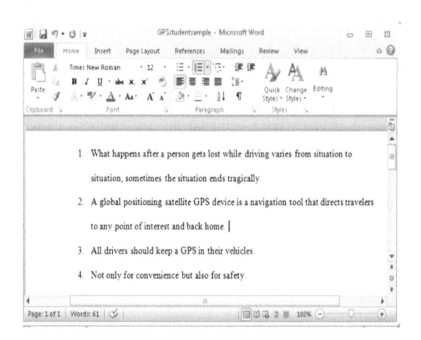

Step 4: Print out only the page that contains your isolated sentences.

STAGE TWO: ANALYZING SENTENCES INDIVIDUALLY

ANALYZE

The second stage of the proofreading system is to analyze each of your isolated sentences for completeness and clarity. Allow approximately five to seven minutes per paragraph to complete this stage.

Step 1: With a blank sheet of paper, cover every sentence except the last one on your printed page. Slowly read it aloud, adding the words *I realize* to the beginning of the sentence. This technique will help you hear if you have omitted any words and help you see if you have typed any words that are different from what you intended to type.

Step 2: Ask, "Is this a complete thought?" Do **not** uncover the sentences before it. The individual sentence you are focusing on must be a complete thought that makes total sense all by itself. If it does not, write a zero in front of it.

0	4. Not only for convenience but also for safety.

Step 3: If it is a complete thought, then ask, "Is this a clear sentence?" If the answer is yes, write a checkmark in front of it. If the answer is no, write a one in front of it.

1	2. A global positioning satellite GPS device is a navigation tool that directs travelers to any point of interest and back home.
√	3. All drivers should keep a GPS in their vehicles.
0	4. Not only for convenience but also for safety.

Step 4: Finally, ask yourself, "Is this sentence really two (or more) sentences crammed together?" If the answer is yes, write a two in front of it.

2	1. What happens after a person gets lost while driving varies from situation to situation, sometimes the situation ends tragically.
1	2. A global positioning satellite GPS device is a navigation tool that directs travelers to any point of interest and back home.
√	3. All drivers should keep a GPS in their vehicles.
0	4. Not only for convenience but also for safety.

Step 5: Repeat the above three steps, asking the same three questions with the next-to-last sentence.

- Is it complete?
- Is it clear?
- Is it not crammed into another one?

Continue this three-step analysis with each isolated sentence in reverse order until you end up at your first sentence last.

Congratulations! You have already finished proofreading all of your sentences with checkmarks in front of them.

STAGE THREE: CORRECTING SENTENCES INDIVIDUALLY

The third stage of the proofreading process is to correct the sentences with a zero, one, or two written in front of them. The amount of time that it will take to make these corrections will vary from five minutes to an hour or more, depending upon the number of errors and your prior knowledge base.

Step 1: Correct all incomplete sentences with a zero written in front of them. They are fragments, rather than full sentences. If you can tell what information is missing, then add it to make the sentence complete. If you are unable to correct these errors, then you will need to take the time to work through Chapter 1 of this book.

Step 2: Correct all sentences with the number one written in front of them. These sentences may be unclear due to imprecise words, pronoun shifts, inconsistent lists, or incorrect punctuation marks. To correct these errors, do the following:

- Change vague words into specific ones.

    - ☹ **Everybody** has **things** to do and **stuff**.

    - ☺ College students have classes to attend and homework to finish.

- Make the number of people in the sentence consistent.

    - ☹ A **student** has to submit **their** homework on the due date.

    - ☺ **Students** have to submit **their** homework on the due date.

- Make items in a list consistent by working through Chapter 3.

- Separate extra information from the main thought of the sentence by working through Chapter 4.

If you have previously worked through these chapters, you may need to refer to the second and third major purposes for punctuation in the Quick Guide at the end of this book.

Step 3: Correct all sentences with the number two written in front of them. These are run-on sentences, meaning two complete sentences are crammed into each other with no punctuation mark or only a comma between them. To find out how to make these corrections, work through Chapter 2. If you have previously worked through that chapter, you may need to refer to the first purpose for punctuation in the Quick Guide at the end of this book.

STAGE FOUR: RETURNING SENTENCES TO PARAGRAPH FORM FOR THE FINAL POLISH

The last stage of the proofreading system is to return your sentences to paragraph form for the final polishing. Allow approximately two minutes per paragraph to complete this stage.

Step 1: Now that you have proofread and corrected every sentence of the last paragraph in your paper, place your cursor in front of the last sentence and press the backspace key as many times as needed until it is one space after the previous period. Repeat with each sentence. This action deletes the numbers and puts your sentences back together. The following example illustrates how this looks in Microsoft Word.

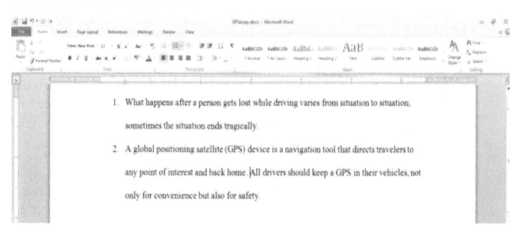

Step 2: After deleting the number one and backspacing to the margin, press the tab key one time. Your sentences are now back together as a properly indented paragraph. The following example illustrates how this looks in Microsoft Word. Be sure to save your work before going on to the next step.

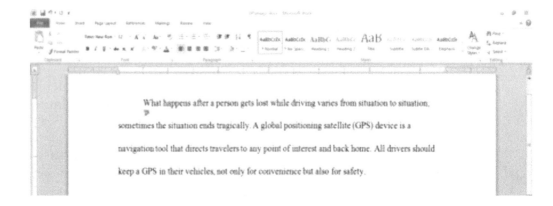

What happens after a person gets lost while driving varies from situation to situation.

sometimes the situation ends tragically. A global positioning satellite (GPS) device is a

navigation tool that directs travelers to any point of interest and back home. All drivers should

keep a GPS in their vehicles, not only for convenience but also for safety.

Step 3: Repeat all four stages of the proofreading process (isolating, analyzing, correcting, returning) with every paragraph in your paper, working in reverse order so that you finish your first paragraph last. Save your work every time you complete this process with an individual paragraph.

Step 4: Print out your complete, corrected paper and slowly read it aloud from beginning to end to make sure that you made all the changes you intended and ensure that it reads smoothly and clearly. This is your last chance to polish your work and make it shine, so take your time. When finished, save your work.

Congratulations! Now that you have worked through all the steps in this four-stage proofreading system, you have caught and corrected many more errors than you would have if you had simply done the last step, which is generally the only step that most people do when they proofread. Keep up the good work.

APPENDIX

Reviewing Quick Guides

For your review, this appendix contains the following three Quick Guides:

1. Three Major Purposes for Punctuation
2. Three Minor Purposes for Punctuation
3. Four Stages of Proofreading

Three Major Purposes for Punctuation

PUNCTUATION PURPOSE #1

To **separate two complete sentences**, choose one of these three rules:

1. Put a period **between** the two sentences.

Example: This sentence is short. It is followed by a slightly longer sentence.

2. Put a semicolon **between** the two sentences.

Example: This sentence is short; it is followed by a slightly longer sentence.

Example: This sentence is short; moreover, it is followed by a slightly longer sentence.

3. Put a comma **before** a coordinating conjunction (for, and, nor, but, or, yet, so) between the two sentences.

Example: This sentence is short, but the second sentence is longer and appears after a coordinating conjunction.

PUNCTUATION PURPOSE #2

To **separate items in a list**, follow these three rules:

1. When the list is **within** the sentence, put commas between the items.

Example: Our new officers are Bill, Jean, Charlie, and Tiffany.

2. When the list is **after** the sentence, separate the sentence from the list with a colon.

Example: Our new officers are the following people: Bill, Jean, Charlie, and Tiffany.

3. When there is a list within a list, **alternate** the comma and the semicolon.

Example: Our new officers are Bill, president; Jean, vice-president; Charlie, secretary; and Tiffany, treasurer.

PUNCTUATION PURPOSE #3

To **separate extra information** from the sentence, follow these four rules:

1. When the extra information is **before** the sentence, put a comma between the introduction and the sentence.

Example: Jean, please punctuate this sentence.

Example: After a lengthy amount of deliberation, Jean punctuated the sentence.

Example: According to the author, "Punctuating sentences is fun."

2. When the extra information **slightly interrupts** the sentence, put a pair of commas around the interrupter.

Example: The length of a sentence, however, does not determine punctuation rules.

Example: "Punctuating sentences," claims the author, "is fun."

3. When the extra information **strongly interrupts** the sentence, put a pair of parentheses or a pair of dashes around the interrupter.

Example: Punctuating sentences—believe it or not—is easy to do.

Example: Punctuating sentences (believe it or not) is easy to do.

4. When the extra information is **after** the sentence, use a comma if the extra information needs no emphasis, a dash if it needs emphasis, or a colon if it is an explanation.

Example: Please punctuate this sentence, Jean.

Example: "Punctuating sentences is fun," claims the author.

Example: There is only one good reason for missing class—death.

Example: There is only one good reason for missing class: death.

PUNCTUATION PURPOSE #4

To identify **quotes**, follow these five rules:

1. Place quotation marks **around** the exact words someone said.

Example: John told Mary, "I love you more than anyone else."

2. Place single quotation marks **around** a quote within a quote.

Example: Mary said, "Get lost, John. I overheard you tell Lisa, 'You are my one true love.'"

3. Place the colon **after** a complete sentence to introduce a long quote.

Example: C.S. Lewis describes an imaginary creature called a marsh-wiggle:

> He had very long legs and arms, so that although his body was not much bigger than a dwarf's, he would be taller than most men when he stood up. The fingers of his hands were webbed like a frog's, and so were his bare feet which dangled in the muddy water. He was dressed in earth-colored clothes that hung loose about him.

4. Use the ellipsis to show that a word or words are **missing** in a quote.

Example: C.S. Lewis points out, "The fingers of his hands were webbed...and so were his bare feet."

5. Use brackets to show that a word or words have been **added** in a quote.

Example: C.S. Lewis points out, "The fingers of his [the marsh-wiggle's] hands were webbed like a frog's, and so were his bare feet."

PUNCTUATION PURPOSE #5

To identify **numbers**, follow these four rules:

1. Place the hyphen **between** the words of two-digit compound numbers.

Example: There were twenty-one candles on her birthday cake.

2. Place the comma in **front** of every third digit from the end in numbers 1,000 and higher.

Example: The bookstore ordered 1,230,000 books last year.

3. Place the colon **between** hours and minutes and between chapters and verses.

Example: Many college classes begin at 8:00.

Example: One familiar scripture verse is John 3:16.

4. Place the dollar sign in **front** of numbers to identify money and a decimal point between the dollars and the cents.

Example: The book costs $79.95.

PUNCTUATION PURPOSE #6

To identify **titles**, follow these two rules:

1. Italicize the title of an entire work and place quotation marks **around** titles of parts inside the work.

Example: "Puddleglum" is the fifth chapter in C.S. Lewis's book *The Silver Chair*.

2. Place a colon **between** a title and a subtitle.

Example: She has watched *Star-Trek: Enterprise* at least five times.

Four Stages of Proofreading

ISOLATE

Step 1: Click the cursor in front of the last paragraph of your paper.

Step 2: Click on the numbering icon in the menu bar.

Step 3: Press the enter key after every period in the paragraph.

Step 4: Print out the page of isolated sentences.

ANALYZE

Step 1: Cover all other sentences and read the last sentence.

Step 2: If the sentence does not make complete sense by itself, write a zero in front of it.

Step 3: If the sentence is clear and complete, write a checkmark in front of it. If the sentence is complete but not clear, write a one in front of it.

Step 4: If the sentence is really two (or more) sentences crammed together, write a two in front of it.

Step 5: Repeat steps 2-4 with each sentence, working in reverse order.

CORRECT

Step 1: Correct all sentences with a zero written in front of them by adding the missing part (see Chapter 1).

Step 2: Correct all sentences with a one written in front of them by making them clear (see Chapter 4). If any of the sentences contains a list, make the items consistent (see Chapter 3).

Step 3: Correct all sentences with a two written in front of them by separating them (see Chapter 2).

RETURN

Step 1: Place your cursor in front of each corrected sentence and backspace until the sentence is no longer isolated.

Step 2: Press the tab key at the beginning of the first sentence to indent the paragraph.

Step 3: Repeat all four stages with every paragraph in the essay.

Step 4: Slowly read your complete, corrected essay aloud.

CPSIA information can be obtained
at www.ICGtesting.com
Printed in the USA
LVOW02s2335060817
543357LV00002B/2/P